WHAT I LEARI
THE RAN

AND OTHER STORIES
WEST TEXAS CHI

TEXAS HERITAGE SERIES:
NUMBER TWO

WHAT I LEARNED ON THE RANCH
AND OTHER STORIES FROM A WEST TEXAS CHILDHOOD

James Bruce Frazier

Foreword by Donald S. Frazier

McWhiney Foundation Press
McMurry University
Abilene, Texas

Library of Congress Cataloging-in-Publication Data

Frazier, James Bruce.
      What I learned on the ranch and other stories from a
      West Texas childhood / by James Bruce Frazier.
      p. cm. -- (Texas heritage series ; no. 2)
      ISBN 1-893114-43-0 (alk. paper)
  1. Frazier, James Bruce--Childhood and youth. 2. Ranch
life--Texas, West. 3. Depressions--1929--Texas, West. 4. Texas,
West--Social conditions. 5. Texas, West--Social life and cus-
toms. I. Title: What I learned on the ranch. II. Title. III. Series.
      F392.W43F73 2003
      976.4'062--dc22

              2003018522

McWhiney Foundation Press
McMurry Station, Box 637
Abilene, TX 79697-0637
(325) 793-4682
www.mcwhiney.org

Printed in the United States of America

ISBN 1-893114-43-0
10 9 8 7 6 5 4 3 2 1

Book Designed by Rosenbohm Graphic Design

CONTENTS

FOREWORD
STORIES FROM MY DAD

What I Learned on the Ranch is a collection of the childhood reminiscences of my dad, James Bruce Frazier, who was a curly headed kid back in the 1920s and 30s. They are set on the Cross Ell Ranch in Howard County, Texas, just west of the city limits of Big Spring and just south of present-day Interstate 20. These stories, chock full of colorful anecdotes and interesting turns of phrase, were staples of my childhood and have proven a rich legacy enjoyed even now by the great-grandchildren of the author.

There are a few things the reader must know about my dad and me. First of all, he was the father of three daughters and seven sons, of whom I am the youngest. As a result, I have a view and memory of my dad from the tail end of a large family — I am sure my oldest brother's twenty extra years on earth give him a completely different vision. I can't speak to that, but I can tell you what I know about my dad. He was forty-one when I was born, and he was a true West Texas original.

He was born January 13, 1924, in Electra, Texas, near Wichita Falls. He moved to the Cross Ell Ranch just west of Big Spring in 1927 with his parents to run the cotton and cattle operation, but his grandfather, James Thompson Frazier, actually owned it. My dad lived there until they moved to town sometime around 1935. The remnants of the Cross Ell are still in the family, but the richest portion of those acres is contained in these pages.

While I was growing up in Arlington — that "city of cul-de-sacs" as writer Larry McMurtry has described it — I was always a little uneasy about my own roots. First of all, my friends had fathers who had long corporate careers with such uninteresting yet safe-sounding places as The Associates or General Dynamics. They were financial bureaucrats or defense industry functionaries, and they went to work in the morning and they came home at night, just like they had done for a decade or two. My dad was different. When asked what my dad did for a living, I responded to the questioner by saying "he is a training director." It sounded settled, respectful, safe, and he was a trainer — for American Manufacturing in Fort Worth. As I grew up, though, I learned he was so much more.

One of my earliest childhood memories was leaving Big Spring when I was nearly four. I did not learn until later what the circumstances were surrounding that move — so mysterious to me at the time — but I always knew there was a kind of sadness surrounding it. Big Spring was home country to my family, a home country that I really never knew. From there, we moved to exotic places like Eagle Pass and San Antonio, Macon, Georgia, and ultimately to Arlington. The gap in my family heritage, for me, was about Big Spring. Everyone in my family seemed to have a rich memory of this place but me.

My dad died in 1989 when he was sixty-five and I was twenty-four. One of our toughest tasks as a family was to encapsulate his life into a brief obituary. Most postings of this sort start with the person's name and occupation. That was a little tough to do for my dad. He had been a lot of things in his life. He had been a West Texas ranch kid whose heroes were cowboys. He had been a town urchin in Big Spring after the family left the Cross Ell. He had been a very proud Texas Aggie, and he had served in World War II in the Z.I., or Zone of the Interior, and had been sent home to the dry climate of West Texas to either die of pneumonia or to recover from it. He had passed on jobs being a meteorologist for Continental Airlines and an animator for Disney and went back to Texas A&M to continue his education and to teach returning G.I.s farming techniques as they transitioned into peacetime jobs. He also married a lifelong school friend and occasional sweetheart, Jimmie Faye Rogers.

Big Spring always called him home. While my three oldest siblings were born in Bryan, the rest of us are natives of that sun-baked and scruffy country in the shadow of Scenic Mountain, South Mountain, and Signal Peak. This was my dad's natural element.

Like many West Texans or fathers of large families, dad was always hustling and thinking up new projects that were going to be either a) lucrative or b) good for the community. He carried into most of his outings the fearlessness and optimism that all would end well, and he engaged in many endeavors typical of his time and place. He farmed cotton and dabbled with raising livestock. He taught geology and agriculture at the local junior college. He also had a few adventures that might seem unconventional to today's observer. He had a local radio and television show. He ran an ambulance service. He sold Christmas trees. He led tours to Europe or helped locate missing Americans in Mexico. He hunted meteorites (some of which I saw displayed much later at Texas Christian University). He wrote articles for magazines and newspapers. He even tried owning a nursing home so that the elderly of Big Spring did not have to leave town to find care. He was a ceaseless booster for Big Spring. Eventually, luck and optimism could no longer sustain him in his home country. That time came when I was nearly four.

These stories came to be, I believe, because my dad was trying to recapture his lost sense of place and to deal with his new sense of rootlessness as he left Big Spring for good. At the same time he was passing on his West Texas ranch heritage to his kids. This, of course, was a mystery to me as I grew up among the asphalt and soccer field landscape of Arlington and the Dallas-Fort Worth Metroplex, just then having its own rural past buried under its present-day urban/suburban jumble.

Now that fate has landed me back in West Texas — in Abilene — I think I more fully understand what he was doing. Like my dad, more people than not end up leaving this part of the country and wind up raising their kids in cul-de-sacs somewhere east of the Brazos. As a result, there is a longing for roots that reach deep, a yearning for wide vistas and days without smog and haze. While my older brothers and sisters have rural and small town childhood memories of their own, I and those of us toward the back end of what my mother called "the second family" had none. Dad wrote these stories to help fix that.

He called these stories by several names, among them "Stories for a Seventh Son" and "Everyone Needs a Ranch." I think the latter is the most revealing. To my dad, a long way from his Howard County home and watching his younger children grow up in a very different place, this became a canon of life. And, as was typical of his generous and hospitable nature, if you didn't have a ranch experience of your own while growing up, he'd happily loan you his.

Donald S. Frazier
Abilene, Texas

CROSS ELL HOME

On a spring day in 1927 skies were overcast. We were moving in a Model T Ford coupe from Electra, Texas, three hundred unpaved miles to the western town of Big Spring. The last forty miles crossed Iatan Flat in rain-filled ruts cut deep in sticky red clay.

In Big Spring, Main Street ran north and south and the highway, US Number 1, crossed from east to west. The Model T turned right at the court house square and went two blocks to the Railroad Tracks then made a U turn doubling back past the State National Bank and came to a stop in front of Fox Drug Store. Mama, Daddy, Baby Sister and I took shelter from the rain under the wooden awning.

We were moving from the Burkburnett oil fields to Big Spring, our new home for a lot longer than anyone could have guessed on that dreary day. Inside the Fox Drug Store we sat at a little round table with twisted wire legs and ordered three fountain Cokes. Baby Sister, snug in her blanket, had her bottle and was more asleep than awake. Daddy had business to attend to, so I looked outside at rain falling on the street intersection.

Golf bags and clubs filled the display window. The wooden floor resounded as people crossed toward a marble-top fountain. If they talked, I don't remember it, only what my eager eyes recorded in my memory, my first adventure, coming to the Cross Ell Ranch.

Long after the Cokes were gone, we returned to the car and headed out of town west toward El Paso, downhill from the red, sandstone courthouse into a flood-filled place called Jones Valley that was more like a lake on that day. People were trying to live in tents with water up to their knees or paddle to their houses in boats. On the north side of the highway, steam switch engines made waves as they ran through water covering the tracks. It came near the fireboxes, and if it poured inside, the trains couldn't run.

I felt sorry for people whose houses and tents were surrounded by water, but soon we crossed to the other side climbing a hill out of the mess on our way to the Cross Ell Ranch. It took a long time to cover those four miles from the courthouse to the faded red front gate. We drove through thickets of mesquite trees and down into a water lot with a concrete horse trough where the animals came to drink.

Cows lay munching or standing in little bunches huddling against the rain. Beyond the water lot were corrals, a dipping vat, and the biggest used-to-be red barn in the whole county.

The Model T turned south past corrals, past out-buildings, many iron plows and wagons, stopping in front of a weathered pine lumber house, gray like all the buildings, corrals, wagons and anything made of wood. Behind it was a smoke house and in front a tank-shack built near two windmills. One was wood and the other was bright-colored metal that made a ringing noise as the sucker rods went up and down.

There were two rows of chinaberry trees in front of the house and a barbed wire fence to keep the livestock out of the yard. In the middle of the front porch was an underground cistern filled by gutters that collected rainfall from the roof. The top of the house was protected by several lovely lightning rods, each fitted with a metal musket bayonet pointing at the sky, and arrow shaped wind veins with stars cut in purple glass on the feather end. There were colored glass balls below and twisted metal rods running down into the ground to direct lightning away from the roof.

The old house had seen better days. The cistern overflowed from the long spell of rains, and the wooden front door was hanging by a single hinge. It had two holes blown through the center panel by a double-barreled shotgun. Rain was falling into the living room through a huge hole in the roof.

Daddy set up my little iron bed in the living room just out of reach of the drip water, and Mama tucked me into fresh warm bedclothes. I was asleep in no time at all. Later in the night I awoke. The rain had stopped and through the hole bright moonlight streamed in from a sky filled with stars. I was at home, for the rest of my life.

CROSS ELL PEOPLE

Daylight is important on the ranch. Work begins and ends with it. Lamps help extend working time, but coal oil gives a soft gentle light that does not encourage work. It will pass to get clothes on, breakfast started, and chores begun, but daylight is for serious work.

Daddy took me to the barn as soon as it was light enough to see. There we met Mr. Callihan, who was busy harnessing Babe and Pete, a team of mules. All the cows had been milked and the livestock fed, breakfast past, and the tools laid out for a day's work.

Daddy said, "Son, this is Mr. Callihan, our renter, who lives in the white house and works the field on the west part of the ranch." He lived there with his wife Sally and their kids Ross, Geneva, Lillian, and Leon. His first name was Sam. "The corrals on the west side of the barn are his."

I was timid and didn't know what to say. Daddy told me to give him my right hand, so I did, and he shook it warmly. Mr. Callihan was the nicest man I had met, and probably the first time I had ever been introduced to anyone as a real person. He wore a straw hat with a wide brim, clean blue overalls, and fresh blue shirt. His face was smooth and he smiled like it came directly from his heart. His eyes twinkled and he made me feel like I was somebody. I loved him from the moment I saw him and all the rest of my life.

There were other families on the Cross Ell. Arthur Hartman stayed on the land with his wife "Old Doodler" and her son Verl. They lived in a white house in the north pasture, between the prairie dog town and a grain field. Old Doodler was fat, she could play the guitar and dance barefoot in the front yard, and knew all the sad songs about cowboys and railroad engineers. She could also drive a team and grub mesquite stumps for fire wood. Verl was her boy by another man, but Mr. Hartman treated him like his own son. When he was big enough Verl joined the service as a gunner and got killed when his B-10 Martin Bomber crashed in California in 1938.

Cross Ell people came in a variety of colors, languages, sizes, and styles of living. Some were old and some were kids like me. Some were big and strong, and some were sick and crippled.

Snookey was black, and he was my friend. Luis was brown, and we spoke Spanish together. Ross and Verl and Leon were white and bigger than me. Grace was blind; she did the washing.

Daddy and Mr. Hartman and Mr. Callihan were grown men, strong, with the voice of authority, sunburned skin all the way up to where their hats shaded their faces. In church it was easy to tell who were ranchers and farmers, and who were bankers and druggists, when they took their hats off. The bankers and druggist had pale faces, but the farmers and ranchers had faces with the top half white and the bottom half brown.

When you look closely at folks they are all different in some ways and alike in others. They all cry when someone they loves dies, or when they get hurt. All get hungry, and all like fried chicken, or a watermelon broken open and eaten in the field, and coffee and bacon and biscuits in the morning. People share many things in common. When a thundershower comes up and big raindrops begin to fall, they all run for cover — black, white, and brown, old folks and kids, the blind lady, and everybody caught out in the storm. We share much in common.

On the Cross Ell there was a place for every creature, man and beast. All were needed and all had a job to do because it was a working ranch. Men did heavy work like plowing, tending cattle, chopping wood. Kids did chores, gathered wood and kindling, hunted turkey nests, and gathered eggs.

Each person also had their own cotton sack. Kids' sacks were smaller, but there were no black or brown sacks, just sacks to be filled with cotton in the fall. There were long-handled hoes and short-handled hoes. At chopping time you got a hoe that fit your size, not your color or your language. Hoes talk only the language of work.

When evening came and the were chores done, the supper dishes washed, dried and put away in the cupboard, we would sit on the porch and watch the stars come out.

> *Star light, star bright,*
> *First star I see tonight,.*
> *I wish I may, if I might,*
> *Have this wish I wish tonight.*

Every summer night we would repeat that little verse as greeting to the first star we would see. Some of those wishes came true, and some we forgot, but the wishes had the same power over each of us — Luis, Snookey, Baby Sister, Ross, Verl, Leon, and me. Wishes don't have any color either.

We sang songs in the twilight. Sometimes we would go up to the Callihan house where Mr. Callihan would resin his fiddle bow and play the old tunes — *Casey Jones, Bury Me Not on the Lone Prairie, Swing Low Sweet Chariot, Clementine, The Wreck of Number Nine, Little Joe the Wrangler, Tumbling Tumbleweeds, Home on the Range, Rancho Grande, Cieleto Lindo, Rock of Ages, Buffalo Gals,* and the fiddle breakdowns, *Turkey in the Straw, Twenty Third of January,* and *Leather Britches,* and yodeling songs like *Blue Yodel Number Nine.*

There were sad songs that brought tears to our eyes — *Streets of Laredo* and *Tom Dooley* — and happy songs that made us want to shout, like *When the Saints Go Marching In.* We sang them all before anyone had electricity.

We were the Cross Ell people who made quilts together from tiny scraps of cloth. Nothing was wasted, not a bit of string, piece of wire, feathers, or old bacon grease. Everything had uses, and we knew how to use everything.

Cross Ell people made lye soap from old grease. We butchered, caned, and pickled. We forged our own branding irons, put leather on worn-out boots, mended harnesses and saddles, built chicken coops, gates, and toys for the children. Old and young depended on each other without any talk about a generation gap. We spent our lives together under God's great sky in the sun, rain, dust, and the ice of winter.

When one would die, like Uncle Jonah, a black cowhand, they made a box, dug a hole, and buried him in the pasture. We all cried, the white ladies cried, the black ladies cried, and the Spanish ladies cried, and all of us kids cried and cried. We had lost our friend and he took a little part of our lives with him when he crossed over Jordan.

Jonah worked at what he knew best, a gentle hand with horses, calves, and baby pigs. He made reed whistles for the kids, and sometimes moonshine whiskey for everybody. We missed him and loved him.

Sooner or later we will all sleep in the same ground we came from, where there are no languages or colors, just God's children resting together.

THE
CROSS ELL BRAND

One day early on, as I walked along with my father around the corrals and over to the little stock pond choked with cattail rushes, I asked him, "Daddy, why do they call this the Cross Ell Ranch?"

He told me, "Because that is the cattle brand we use. We burn it into the hide on the left hip of cows on this ranch. It is the letter ell with a cross bar half way up. Some folks call it the Bar Ell, but we call it the Cross Ell." All ranches have their own brands to identify property. Those who use the same mark place it on different parts of the cow so as to not confuse ownership. "They also ear mark cattle, in addition to the brand," he added. "The Cross Ell cuts a swallow fork in the right ear."

Later, I watched as Ross and Verl and Leon wrestled a yearling calf on the dusty ground in the corral. Leon roped him with one quick flick of his wrist and let him run until he reached the end of the lasso that he had wrapped around a post set in the center of the cow lot. The poor dogie turned a flip as he hit the end of it. Verl grabbed the tail in both hands and Ross fell on his head with one hand around his muzzle and the other full of ear.

Verl switched from tail to feet, holding one back hoof with both hands and from a sitting position he braced both his boots against the other back foot of the calf, stretching them apart, and Verl leaned back in a sitting position in the dirt.

Ross sat back in a fresh cow pile and stretched the front end of the calf in the opposite direction with the help of the rope snubbed to the post. That calf lay helpless on the ground. The poor critter could only roll his dust-covered eyes and bawl for his mother as Mr. Hartman came over with the red-hot iron. First there was the letter ell that burned the hair and then into the hide, and then a second iron burned the ell into a cross.

There is no other smell that is exactly like the one made by a white-hot branding iron, nor a sound like when it burns through the curly Hereford hair. Dust and smoke mix into a haze over the corral during this operation.

The calf is released and quickly regains its feet and runs to the far corner of the pen huddling with the other yearlings who have just been branded. Each animal will bear the scar for the rest of its life, and that mark — the Cross Ell — identifies it forever as being from that ranch.

Each ranch has its own cattle brand, and that is how it is known all over the country, depending on the importance of the ranch and where the cattle go. The brands are registered in the county courthouse and are the personal property of the ranch owners and are willed to their descendants.

Many a cowboy makes his way in life never knowing how to read and write, yet none is so ignorant that he can't make the mark of his boss's ranch or read those brands on the cattle he works.

When he makes that mark with a white-hot iron in living flesh, he knows what it means. This lesson is learned early in ranch life even before children start to school. When they eventually do venture off the property, they remember where they come from. Ranch kids belong to the R Bar, the B Backward F, the Rocking W, or in this case the Cross Ell.

"Who are you, kid?" "I'm from the Cross Ell."

Folks say things like, "That Cross Ell boy is taking the Lazy Eleven girl to the Old Settlers Reunion."

There is something respectable about belonging to a certain ranch. Everyone knew the school bus picked up the R Bar kids and it was a full load. They were mostly cousins and kids of families who worked the R Bar, but quite a number were brothers and sisters. There were enough of them to make folks in town take notice.

History was told by cattle brands. A cow or bull with four or five brands let people know that this animal had been around. The cow had dropped calves on several ranches, or the bull had sired descendants all over the territory. This way people kept up with bloodlines, avoiding inbreeding.

A cowboy applying for work would rattle off the ranches where he had worked, and one could check into his character by asking around those ranches. Was he honest, a hard worker, or lazy? Could he break horses, handle a team? Did he drink a lot of whiskey, or spend time in jail?

Cattle brands made an impression on more than the animals that wore them. They set the character of the country and gave folks something to be proud of. It didn't have to be such a large ranch, just good, clean, and honest. Boys and girls liked to bring honor and respect to the one they belonged to, long after they moved to town and faraway places.

It was nice to be a part of something. It defined who one was and set the boundaries of their territory.

MY FIRST HAIRCUT

Leadford Hogue gave me my first haircut, and he won the Silver Star. Oh, the Silver Star was something he got in World War II, a long time after he cut my hair. Really those are two different stories, but that's how I always thought of Leadford — my haircut and his medal for bravery in the South Pacific at the first of the war.

The Hogue family was kin to Sally Callihan, so I guess Leadford and his little brother Bruce were cousins to the Callihans.

Times were hard in 1927 and the Hogues came to the ranch to help Sam Callihan with his farming. They lived in the line shack or, as we called it, The Shack. It was a three room house built flat on the ground with a flat roof, one door, and four windows. The walls were boxing planks going up and down with narrow bats nailed over the cracks where the boards met. That kept the wind and rain out, most of the time. Someone tacked newspapers over the inside walls and that helped keep out the wind where the boards warped, and someone colored the faces of people whose pictures were in the papers and filled all the A's and O's with either blue or red Crayola. It made the walls look like somebody cared enough to add some color.

Inside were three plain rooms without cupboards or storage cabinets. The south side was divided into two rooms and on the north a long room ran the length of the shack with a window in each end. The north was solid wall because that's the direction the wind blew when northers hit in winter and sand blew during dust storms. It was not a fancy place to live, without any water or an outhouse. People threw bottles and cans out back in a mesquite and prickly-pear thicket. That's where Leadford, who was older than me, and Bruce, who was just a little kid, lived.

Their mama and daddy worked in the fields like all grown folks on the Cross Ell, which left us kids to play by ourselves after chores and until dinner time, and then afternoons until milking time and supper. When we were little we had lots of time to do keen things like drowning out ground squirrels, catching doodle-bugs, and playing in the dirt.

It was one of those bright summer days when Baby Sister and I wandered up to the shack and found Leadford and Bruce sitting on the two chairs leaning back against the wall on either side of the doorway. We said "howdy" just like grown folks do and started talking about june bugs and chickens and things.

After a while Leadford said to me, "You and Baby Sister both look like girls with her straight cotton hair, cut with bangs across the front, and your head full of long curls."

Now he was a big boy, eight years old and I was nearly four, so I respected what he said. That was not the first time someone had told me I looked like a little girl. Two big boys working at the Dr. Pepper Bottling Works in town said it just the week before when we went there to see Mr. Stalcup, who lived upstairs over the plant. We were playing with his little girl, Patsy Ruth, when those old boys said, "Lookie, there are three little girls playing with the soda water caps!"

I put my hands on my hips and looked right at them and said, "I'm not a little girl, I'm a boy!"

They whistled and shouted, "Who-ee! You could have fooled me with those pretty long curls. Does your mama know you're a boy? You better go tell her, quick!"

I was still mad about that and all the rest of the stuff they said, and now Leadford was talking about it, too.

He said, "Yes sir, you sure do look like a girl. What you need is a haircut so you'll look like me and Bruce."

I wasn't too happy with the idea of looking like Bruce — he hardly had any hair — and Leadford's head

had hair on top but his neck was shaved up higher than the top of his ears. He had a point, though. No one would ever think he or his little brother were girls.

Leadford went on talking about my long curls until I was sick of hearing it. He said, "I know all about hair cuts and barbering. I'm gonna grow up and be a barber some day."

He said, "I can cut your hair right now if you want me to."

Boy, did I! That was the answer to what was bothering me most in the whole world, that day. I asked, "You could do it right now?"

"Sure as shootin'," he replied.

In no time he found his mama's barber shears and clippers and a comb with fine teeth on one end and course teeth on the other. I sat in one of the chairs out there in the yard, and he took his time squinting his eyes and with his mouth shut tight and the tip of his tongue sticking out, he snip, snip, snipped off my long curls and one by one they fell on the hard-packed earth in the yard. He combed a little bit and cut more off the sides and top and clipped up my neck and over the ears. At last he put his tools away, and I looked in their cracked mirror and, sure enough, I didn't look like a little girl anymore. I looked like Leadford!

I was so proud of myself I caught Baby Sister by the hand and ran back to the house to show Mama. That was my big mistake! Mama cried, and cried and cried some more, saying things about her baby's beautiful golden curls and a lot of stuff I couldn't understand because of her taking on. She marched me by the hand right back up to the shack, and she nearly scared Leadford out of his wits. He thought she was going to wallop him or something even worse, and she might have, but she saw my hair all over the yard, and she fell on hands and knees and picked it up, curl by curl, out of the weeds and brush, saving it in her apron.

She cried it all out, and Leadford hung his head and made circles in the dust with his big toe, and then at last we trudged back to the house. I didn't know what she was going to do with all that hair in her apron, but I was scared she would figure some way to put it back on my head. I was thankful to see her stuff it in a box where she kept letters tied with ribbons and other ladies' keepsakes. She grieved over my hair for a long, long time. On Saturday I met Mr. Thomas for the first time in the first real barber shop I had ever been to. He sat me on a board over the arms of his barber chair and shook his head sadly, all the time asking Mama, "What the Sam Hill happened to this kid anyway?"

I was so happy when we stopped by the Dr. Pepper Bottling Plant on the way home so I could show Patsy Ruth and those two big boys that I was not a little girl. Patsy knew it all the time and the big boys weren't there to talk to, but that didn't matter because I knew I wasn't a girl. I was a boy!

The Silver Star Leadford won was not for being a barber. He never did that again as far as I know. He got the medal when his B-17 "Flying Fortress" got its tail shot nearly off out in the Pacific Islands. Leadford was a gunner and he got some wire and spliced the control wires back together before the airplane fell out of the sky. He knew how to do it from fixing barbed wire fences back on the Cross Ell. He said, "I had to fix those wires or fall in the Pacific Ocean, and let me tell you, I don't think I could swim from there back to the ranch."

ROSCOE, ALBERT, AND SAM

Time ran on a set schedule at the Cross Ell Ranch. There were seasons to plant, cultivate, harvest, and prepare land for the next planting time. The full moon and the new moon were important events, and so were Christmas and the Fourth of July. There was "hog killing time" and time to pick peas, time to set hens and times to do all sorts of things. Old folks did these things by the *Farmer's Almanac*.

One of those important things was Saturday bath time, when everyone got clean clothes, and maybe a trip to the store in town, but even more dependable was Sunday. That was the day we went to church.

Everyone had "Sunday-go-to-meeting" clothes, our very best. We were given an envelope and a nickel to seal inside for our offering. On the outside we wrote our names, and checked the boxes that read: "studied your lesson," "daily Bible reader," "on time," "staying for church." If we checked every box at the end we could mark one hundred percent.

That was the high event of every week, and nothing short of death could keep us at home on Sunday morning. Following Sunday school there was the church service —

which we faithfully attended — and Sunday evening services and usually a mid-week service on Wednesday night. When we were older there were youth groups, singings, and summer church camp meetings, all important parts of ranch life.

At home we had a prayer blessing every meal, mother read our *Bible Story Book* at bedtime, and we had prayers before we went to sleep. Those early lessons were well taught and long remembered. Perhaps some of what we learned may have gone a bit beyond what our teachers intended. One I remember best was about the Guardian Angel. Somehow I was convinced that every little kid in the whole world, those on the ranches and even those in the town, were supposed to have a Guardian Angel that followed them around to keep them out of sin and trouble.

At first that was just an interesting story from Sunday school along with Moses and the reed boat in the bull rushes and David who killed the giant Goliath with a stone from his slingshot and the power of God. Now we were taught that each of us had our own personal private angel. I didn't know the scripture that explains all this, but slowly it became firmly fixed in my young mind.

It started out like the other Bible stories learned in classes, but the more I thought about it the better it seemed. Way out there on the wide open spaces of the rangeland and fields, things can get pretty lonesome for a little boy growing up and trying to figure things out for himself. This is especially true when your only constant companion was a baby sister who took long naps. That left lots of time to explore and think about things.

I climbed into the loft of the big old barn and sat looking through the open window across an endless sea of rippling grass dotted with clumps of light green mesquite trees, under an empty sky. There wasn't much to fix my attention until I remembered the story about my very own private Guardian Angel.

That was a grand subject to think about, so I thought about it a lot. What did my Angel look like? Was he a little kid like me? No, he would have to be older and bigger to keep me out of trouble. He must be a grown-up angel of at least fifteen or sixteen. Did he have real wings and fly around above my head looking after me from some invisible place? What was his name? He must have a name.

Little by little I began to figure him out. I began to feel his presence when I was alone, so he must really be somewhere close by. I couldn't quite understand about his wings though, so I reasoned that my invisible Guardian must be floating weightless in the air above me, either with or without wings, it really didn't matter.

Well, I finally had that problem solved. Now it was going to take a lot more thought to come up with his name. As the afternoon wore on the name came to me like an angel whispering in my ear, "My name is Roscoe."

I guess Roscoe was a good and dignified name, perhaps a little unusual, but after all, angels are special beings so why not have a special name?

I was so happy to figure out my Guardian Angel and how he worked that I dropped from the loft through the open trap door into a pile of cotton seed and went outside into the corrals and climbed the gate until I could scramble to the barn roof. I climbed up the easy part to where it got steep, and then holding tight to warped shingles I made my way to the top and walked along the ridge to the ventilator and climbed up on top of that. At last I stood up on the tip top, the highest point on the whole ranch! With a Guardian Angel looking after me I could afford to be daring.

From there I could see across the prairie and the two of us, Roscoe and me, could get to know each other better from our high and airy perch. That was as close to his home in heaven as I could climb, and anyhow, he could just earn his keep by doing his stuff protecting me from falling off the barn roof to certain death in a sea of cow patties. I guess Roscoe knew his business, because none of the shingles came loose on my way down and I didn't fall.

As weeks passed I began to worry about Roscoe. A little boy has so many places to go and so many things to do. Things like catching frogs, watching ants carry crumbs to their nest, looking at baby kittens way back under the house, hunting for hens' nests in the tall weeds. I wondered if Roscoe got tired of following me around all the time.

I spread fresh churned butter onto a piece of bread, sprinkled it with sugar and walked out in the back pasture where the side oats grama was rippling like water on the stock pond in the summer breeze. A hawk circled in search of a rabbit for dinner. I sat down to enjoy my sugar-bread and wished I could share it with Roscoe, who just might be up there circling alongside that hawk in the cloudless sky.

It was then that I realized something else about Roscoe. He had helpers.

It must have been near three o'clock in the afternoon when I just knew he was leaving and someone else had come on duty — his helper, Albert. I couldn't have known it more clearly had Albert whispered it in my ear, but I just knew that Albert worked until eleven and then before midnight, Sam took over.

Well now, that explained everything. The way I had a Guardian Angel all the time was there were three of them working in shifts like the drillers and roughnecks on oil wells, taking turns so drilling never stopped.

So that's how it worked. Roscoe had the day shift, Albert the swing shift, and Sam the graveyard shift. After all, we did live on the Cross Ell Ranch in the middle of the Oil Patch, so it seemed natural and eased my worry lest my angel might get tired. Guardian Angels are supposed to stay awake lest something get you while you sleep. Who knows what's out there in the dark to hurt you?

Guardian Angels make you feel it's safe to shut your eyes and sleep when a thunderstorm is raging just outside your window. Angels are God's messengers. I am thankful to Him for looking after Baby Sister and me and all the little kids on big lonesome ranches.

Once I figured things out, I wasn't afraid. My Guardian Angel and I enjoyed riding bucking horses, swinging from high places, drinking dirty water out of cow tracks, walking in tall grass where there might have been rattlesnakes.

I always knew which one was on duty, and I tried to keep him from getting bored by thinking of things that he could save me from. One thing is for sure: life is more fun when you have Guardian Angels like Roscoe, Albert, and Sam.

THE NIGHT THE
COYOTES CAME

The night the coyotes came, I was sleeping in my little iron bed with the sides that let down. I heard them fighting on the back porch where Daddy hung the sausage, hams, and bacon from the pigs we killed the day before. A whole pack of hungry coyotes were tearing the fresh meat from the hooks where it was cooling out in the crisp November night.

The four glass panes in the window beside my bed were all that separated a little frightened boy from those coyotes in their feeding frenzy. With my head pressed hard against the iron bars I could make out their shapes as they lunged and fought over their feast.

Mama and Daddy were in the kitchen with an oil lamp, and from its glow through the glass in the kitchen door I could make out some of the details of the fight going on so close to me. Daddy opened the door a little crack just big enough to poke the barrel of his big shotgun through.

Blam! Blam! Blam! He shot while Mama held the lamp as close to the glass as she could. Each time he shot, coyotes would howl with pain and scatter only to come back again for the meat. There were so many of them!

When the shells in the shotgun were used up, Mama handed him the Marlin deer rifle and he fired again and again. I could hear the clack-a-clack as he worked the lever to throw out the empty shells. Next morning I found one of the shells in the water bucket and several on the kitchen floor.

After a lot of shooting and coyote howls, it was over. No one opened a door to see the damage until it was good daylight. Then Mama and Daddy found that they had scattered forty sacks of sausage, hams, and bacon all over the south pasture. There were dead coyotes in the yard and behind the house, and the bloody porch was splintered by bullet marks.

I gathered up the red shotgun hulls and cartridge casings. Mama made Baby Sister and me stay in the house all day and didn't let us out of her sight for weeks after.

For a long time I was scared the coyotes would come back and get me, and I dreamed about it, though I took comfort in being inside the house where it was safe in my little iron bed with the sides pulled up around me. They didn't get me that time when I could hear their claws as they ran over the porch floorboards.

I was always scared when I hurried back from the milk pens at dusk. I knew they were waiting for me somewhere out in the mesquite brush. It gave me a cold feeling up the back of my neck!

For a long, long time after that night I had an uneasy feeling they would come back and chase me down and eat me, leaving only my overall buttons for Mama to find in the morning. In school I read stories by Jack London about trappers in the north woods fighting for their lives to escape from timber wolves. In one story a man lost his life to them, and in the spring when the snow melted all they found was his brass belt buckle and hunting knife. I know how scared he was, because I was so frightened myself!

Even now howling wolves and coyotes send shivers down my spine. You never grow too old or brave to forget the night the coyotes came.

RAGGS

Someone was knocking at the kitchen door, and when I opened it there stood a raggedy little man. His shoes didn't completely contain his feet, and though his coat was patched, there were places where his shirt and winter underwear peeked through. Even his face was shaggy with short whiskers and beard mixed, as though he had shaved part of it a week before and left the rest to grow out long.

From his shoulder hung a bundle wrapped in a tattered army blanket secured with binder twine. His pockets were stuffed full of things that made him look lumpy, and his hair was graying and shaggy.

He asked, "Kind sir, can I stay in your barn tonight?"

Daddy came to talk to him and said, "You may stay, but you can't make any fires or smoke in that wooden barn."

The weather was cold, and the raggedy man was smoking a roll-your-own Bull Durham cigarette which he put out and saved behind his ear as he promised not to make any fires or smoke if we let him sleep in the Cross Ell barn.

It made me uneasy to think of sleeping down there with rats, mice, scorpions, snakes, and owls that I knew lived there. Then there were skunks, possums, and spiders I had seen, and imaginary things that just might live in the dark shadows, in corners, or under the boards in the floor. He didn't seem to mind. I guess he had slept in a lot of barns and had come to terms with things that scurry about in the dark.

I never knew his name, but everyone called him Raggs. Mama made him a nice supper of beans, cornbread, and a slice of her yellow pound cake, some coffee, and a glass of milk — just so he wouldn't be tempted to build a cooking fire in the barn, she said.

Raggs seemed happy sitting under the leafless chinaberry tree eating his meal. When he finished he wiped the plate clean with the raggedy edge of his coat and left his dishes on the door step.

Next morning he was up and waiting when we came down to the cow lot at milking time. He helped feed bundles of red-top cane to the animals and washed his face in the horse tank after breaking the thin skim of ice from the top. He turned the spigot and drank water with the same confidence most folks have that water from any tap is drinkable. I wasn't going to tell him that water came from a muddy slime-covered hole in the stock pond that collected gyp-water from the two windmills.

He brought the buckets of milk to the kitchen where Mama strained it through a cup towel. She gave him a breakfast of boiled eggs, sausage, biscuits and coffee. He offered to work for his keep, so she let him chop wood, and I stacked it neatly in the wood box. He saw other odd jobs and offered to do them, and before we knew it Raggs had been hanging around the ranch for several days.

I followed him to hear him tell war stories about fighting Germans when he was in the A.E.F. across the ocean in France. He said he was in the artillery at a place called Verdun, and when I asked him if he killed any Germans, he said, "I reckon I must have."

He explained, "I was a cannon loader on a French 75 field gun, and shots fired by it may have killed people; we never knew for sure, but that's what they were trying to do."

I asked questions, but his answers made me think he must have missed the exciting part of the war that I saw in the picture show. All he told me about was living in a dugout, being in the trenches, cold, wet, muddy, and tired. It didn't sound exciting to hear Raggs tell about it.

There was a tattoo on his arm, a single word, MOTH-ER. I asked and he replied, "I had a mother once. She was a beautiful lady with long black hair, a good Catholic who wore a crucifix and went to Mass, but she died with the flu."

Flu killed a lot of people at the end of the war and in 1919. He had just come home from France when his mother died, so he took to the road and had been riding the rails ever since. "I'm a Knight of the Road," he said.

When Raggs talked about his mother he would get serious and his blue eyes would puddle up with tears that spilled down his sunburned cheeks disappearing into his hairy face. He didn't shave often.

Sometimes while talking about his mother he would take a drink from a bottle wrapped in a paper sack. He cried more when he drank from the sack than he did when he just talked about his mama. He cried a lot for a grown man.

Raggs told me about California, where the sun always shines, and the orange trees grow, and there is a big blue ocean with a beach that goes on forever, and sometimes seals come and lay around. He had been there and seen it all – Hollywood, where the film stars live, and Oregon, with fruit trees and mountains so tall that there's snow on top, even in the summertime. He had seen New Orleans and magnolias and honeysuckle vines.

Raggs had ridden a train with a "Singing Brakeman" named Jimmy Rogers, who could sing and yodel like Old Doodler, the foreman's wife.

"Raggs, where did you stay when you bummed around the country?" I asked.

"In the jungles, kid, in them hobo jungles," he said.

"All along the railroad there are places where hobos sleep and cook and eat. They call them places jungles, but they are not like where Tarzan and the apes lived. They are places where hobos, tramps, and bums stay. They make stew in an old tin can over an open fire. Sometimes the jungles are under bridges or by a river and usually a little ways out of a town, but always close to a railroad."

Inside the army blanket tied with binder twine, Raggs carried a wealth of interesting things — pieces torn from newspapers, old faded and cracked photographs, and a wood carving of a lady with her hands folded and her eyes closed. He said he carved it and it was the Madonna, the mother of Jesus.

I could have it if I had something to give him in return. I offered marbles and my lucky rabbit foot, which was about everything I owned.

He said he would trade it for a full bottle of vanilla extract like Mama used to flavor her pound cake, or maybe some money, or whiskey if I knew where there was any. I didn't have any money, and the only whiskey was in a fruit jar on a high shelf, and the vanilla bottle was almost empty, so we never made a trade.

Raggs didn't stay on the Cross Ell very long, but while he was there he mended saddles, patched the mule's harness and sharpened all the axes and tools on our grinder while I peddled it like a bicycle to make the wheel go around. He was good at fixing things.

One time he cut two pieces of leather in the shape of a shoe and then replaced the bottoms of his worn-through shoes. He punched holes to match the stitches, then he sewed the new leather on to his old shoes and they were ready to go again. He was so smart!

He made new heels for my worn cowboy boots. He cut little pieces of leather in the shape of my old run-over boot heel and stacked one on top of the other like sandwiches, coating each layer with glue. He carved little pieces of wood with sharp ends to spike the layers together, and with nails he hammered the heels back on my boots. Raggs could do almost anything. He said, "Knowing how to do things is like having money in the bank."

He knew songs about *The Big Rock Candy Mountain*, the sad song about Clementine that drowned, and Casey Jones the brave engineer, and *The Old Rugged Cross*. He taught them to me and we sang together. Then I taught him my song, *Jesus Loves Me*, and we sang all the verses.

I told Raggs, "When I grow up, I'm gonna be a hobo, just like you."

He shook his head and began to have tears in his eyes, and said, "Never start life on the open road riding the rails. Son, you got a mama, and a good one too. You got a home on this here ranch. Stay, go to school and learn something, and some day raise a family of your own. Life on the road is not for you."

I wanted to argue with him, but by now he was blubbering so hard that I had to believe what he said, and the life of a hobo was not for me.

Even if I never was going to be a hobo I liked to hear his stories, and he told some good ones. He taught me how to read hobo language on doors and gateposts of houses. One sign meant a free handout and no work, but made just a little different, it meant you had to work for your meal. One mark meant stay away from this place because folks here might turn you over to the law. Another sign means, "There is a mean dog inside this fence."

There were a lot more things that only hobos know, and some things are not even words, like all the railroad signals and lanterns and lights and how different trains have different whistles, and the way a whistle talks, and what the lanterns say — stop, back up, freight on a siding, roll out, and things like that.

There is one whistle for a grade crossing and another for danger. Once when his train was being robbed, the clever engineer signaled that there were robbers on board by whistling the danger signal at every grade crossing. Someone who understood the language of trains had help waiting for them at the next station. When the train stopped they caught the robbers because someone knew whistle language.

Hobos leave messages for each other on the back of signs, inside boxcars, on bridges. I still look for them. Mostly they leave their names, so I always hope I'll see the name Raggs, hoping to see he has been there and is still going, going, going someplace.

There are other names like A Number 1, Hobo King, and of course later on, Kilroy, who had been there before me. All this is a language I knew before I learned real reading and writing, a language they never got around to teaching in school because it's useful only to hobos and railroad men, and little boys who want to know about them.

One day Raggs was gone. When he came he didn't say hello and when he left he didn't say goodbye. I wonder if he was ever really there or did I dream him. Did he settle down, have a home and family, and what was his real name?

When I see a hobo sign beside a door, or a name scrawled on a boxcar, or hear a train whistle in the night, I remember a tattered little veteran of the A.E.F. who taught me the language of trains and hobos and jungles and who cried real tears when I said, "I want to be a hobo like you."

It's better to read about the life of a hobo than to live it, yet I wonder how it would be to travel with the seasons, sleep under the stars, or go to the ocean where seals doze in the sunshine. Raggs made not working for a living sound like fun. Still, I would rather buy shoes in a store than keep patching old ones with scraps of leather. You don't see many hobos nowdays; maybe since we have welfare it doesn't pay to be a hobo any more.

Raggs may have explained their disappearance when he said, "Son, if you have a choice to live rich or live poor, before you choose let me tell you, rich is better!"

THE EAGLES' FATHER

Charlie Bonner's dirty old car came bouncing through the water lot and up to the front gate of the Cross Ell Ranch house and stopped beside the old wooden windmill. I ran as fast as my bare feet would take me over the scorching hot bare earth and around the patches of goat-head stickers. I was always eager to greet Charlie Bonner, who was my father's friend and an all around rascal from the Oil Patch. He always had a surprise for me, and I could hardly wait to see what wonder it was this time.

Once he brought Baby Sister a cup and saucer from the Crawford Hotel Coffee Shop. It said so right on the saucer. One time he gave me the gold owl with ruby eyes right off his watch chain, but when I went to sleep I lost it, and the next time I saw him, he had another just like it. Sometimes he brought me chewing gum. Always it was something interesting, and I could hardly wait to see what he had this day.

Even before he got out of his car, he handed me a cardboard box to carry up to the porch so I could open it in the shade. My heart was pounding with anticipation as we went through the front gate, climbed the rickety steps and sat down beside the cistern on the front porch.

He said, "Be careful how you open it because they're alive and you don't want to scare them."

I was very careful, and as I peeked into the box I could see four eyes glittering at me. As the flaps opened one by one I could see two heads covered with white down, each having a strong curved beak. Beneath each beak was a scrawny neck, a body with bare wings and more white down, and feet with strong looking claws.

"What are they?" I asked, my voice shrill with excitement and wonder.

"Them's baby eagles," Charlie replied. "Baby eagles I rescued from a nest in a power line over in the sand hills by Monahans. You can raise them if you are careful."

"Oh, I'll be careful. I'll be so careful with them. I'll be the eagles' father," I said.

I would have said anything to get to keep two baby eagles all my own. I had never seen any baby eagles. The only tame birds I had seen were canaries at Mrs. Gault's house and the parrot at the Pol Parrot Grocery in town. No one had real eagles. No one but me!

There was no doubt in my mind that I would do everything that was needed to raise my eagles. The only problem I could see was Mama. She took a dim view of raising any other animals besides the ones we had on the Cross Ell Ranch. Each of them had a special place and a special purpose — either to make money, like the beef cattle that went to market, or to save money, like the dogs and cats that kept the rodents down in the grain. It is hard to explain how eagles would do either.

She came out on the porch to look at my new pets and began telling me what a bother two baby eagles would be. I had a counter for every objection, and I clinched my argument by once again saying I would be the eagles' father, and so I won the contest. The eagles could stay. Mr. Bonner left, chuckling about the whole event.

I made a nest for my eagles in an old World War I army helmet, lined with cotton and straw. It was fortunate because my eagles made quite a mess and I would discard the old nest every few days and replace it with fresh materials. The birds ate well and were always hungry. At first I caught grasshoppers and bugs for them, but later on I gave them table scraps, and they consumed biscuits and gravy, peanut butter, scrambled eggs, chicken feed, cow feed, dead rats, and anything I brought them. I would poke whatever I had into their gaping mouths, and they gulped it down. Sometimes they tried to swallow my finger that held the food. Eating was never a problem with those two.

Before long they were too large for the nest, so I moved them into a bushel basket. As they grew they didn't look much like eagles. At first they lost the white down, later they grew pinfeathers that turned out to be dark-colored everywhere except about the neck and head which never did seem to sprout much of anything. The beaks grew larger and sharper, and at last they developed huge wings. They would spread them out either side of the basket and flap them slowly, trying them out for the day when they would soar with other eagles into the sun.

Flight was something that worried me. How could I teach them to fly like a father eagle should be able to do? I need not have worried about that; they were learning a little each day, and I took them out into the chinaberry tree and set them on a branch. They liked the sunshine and stretched their wings and preened their new feathers until they glistened a brilliant black and their necks and heads began to turn pink and later red.

My eagles were never going to grow up to become eagles at all. They were going to be BUZZARDS! I ran down to the barn and crawled into the cotton seed bin and cried for a little while. I didn't want to be The Buzzards' Father. I wanted to be The Eagles' Father.

After a bitter hour of tears, I thought it over. I had been a good father, and I had raised my children, and even if they were buzzards, maybe there is some virtue in being the best father I could be even for two buzzards. They were what they were, and there is a place in this world for both eagles and buzzards.

At last, my children took to the air but returned to sleep in a crowded basket. I stopped feeding them, and they began to hunt for themselves. Finally they didn't come home again. I could see them soaring in the blue Texas sky among the white fluffy clouds, sometimes as tiny specks and sometimes close to the tops of the mesquite trees. I knew they were my children, and this was their home. They cleaned up the dead rabbits on the highway to El Paso, and they ate the dead animals in the pasture, always leaving the earth a little neater than it would have been otherwise. They did what nature intended them to do.

"Charlie Bonner, you rascal," I thought, "I'll bet you knew it all the time." I just know I'm not the only father in the world who set out to raise his children to become eagles and had them turn out to be buzzards. So what? They are first class buzzards, and I am proud of them. After all, I am the buzzards' father.

YOU CAN'T ALWAYS
TELL A MAN

Grandpa said, "Son, before you can become a cowboy, you gotta know more than the cow knows." He spent a lot of time looking at cows and always knew what they were up to, where they went walking and which one was going to find a calf. He knew everything about cows.

"There are two kinds of people on ranches," he told me, "cowboys who spend their money trying to look like cowboys, and those who save their money until they have enough to buy a ranch." Grandpa didn't look like a cowboy. He didn't have to; he owned the ranch.

Some cowboys looked like picture show heroes, spending their wages on shop made boots, a five X beaver Stetson hat, fancy leather belt with a gold buckle, and a saddle of hand-tooled leather, silver conchos and buckles. Most young cowboys grew out of it and went off to pick cotton, roughneck in the oil field, work for the railroad, fight in a war, or join the CCCs, the Civilian Conservation Corps.

Occasionally, drifters came looking for work. Some didn't tarry long enough for us to remember their name, others stayed on for years, even when there was no more work. One of those was Jake, a little fellow, not much bigger than us kids. He worked hard building fences, driving teams, and doctoring stock and kids' cuts and stumped toes. He could break colts to ride or work in a team, always patient and gentle.

Teaching colts to work in harness or under the saddle took time. Mares on the ranch were bred and often had a colt by their side. That's how we replaced work stock. Ranch boys spent hours planning how to break horses to work, but Jake was the master of the art. Some of the boys went to rodeos that featured contests in bronc busting, but I don't remember any of them winning any money at it.

Jake showed up at the Cross Ell with his clothes and tack slung over his back. We had enough hands, but Daddy took pity on him because he was tired, scruffy and dirty, so he let him move in with Uncle Billy and the other cowboys. Jake pulled his weight and drew his pay at the end of the month. Most of the hands drifted on in the fall when the work was done. Jake stayed on picking up a few dollars doing odd jobs for us and the neighbors. He was good at fixing things, going over all the saddles, harness and rigging in the tack room, oiling the leather patching lines, and making metal nose flaps to wean the milk pen calves. On Wednesdays he had a job working at the weekly cattle auction where ranchers from all over West Texas came to buy and sell livestock.

Old Jake hazed the animals through endless corrals, sweating in the summer heat and wrapped up in a greasy old fleece lined canvas jacket in the winter.

He talked to ranchers to see if they had colts to break. Jake would ride for whatever anyone would pay, sometimes ten dollars, but often less. I liked to go along to watch him work because Jake was as good a rider as any.

When he got throwed, he'd land light as a feather and be back on the horse in a minute, trying it all over again. He used to say that old verse, "Ain't never been a horse that couldn't be rode, or a cowboy that couldn't be throwed."

Because Jake was small he could ride like a jockey, all meat and bone with no fat, hard as mesquite wood, and tough as a boot. Come to think of it, Jake was about the color of mesquite wood because he lived out in the weather — wind, sun and, once in a while, rain.

People come and go. Some you remember for one thing and some for another. Jake was dependable and willing to help on any job. He left the Cross Ell and moved to the Lazy Eleven ranch west of the Iatan Flat red beds on the Mitchell County line, in the hills and mesas near Wild Horse Creek. I always looked forward to seeing him at the Wednesday cattle auction where we would "Howdy" each other. When we had colts to break or work stock to train, Jake would be the one we hired. He had a way with animals — they all seemed to remember him as he put them through their paces, obeying his every command.

One Wednesday Mr. Hartman and I were at the auction. I was sitting on the fence looking over a pen of yearlings listening to the chant of Mr. Britton, the auctioneer. Jake came down the alley way driving a bunch of big range steers toward the sale barn. I waved to him and he raised his hand to wave back, but something was wrong because he looked up at me and then on up into the sky, stumbling backward and falling. The frightened steers turned back, stepping all around where he lay in the dirt.

I yelled to Mr. Hartman. He and some other handlers ran to where he lay. Folks said he was bad sick and Mr. Hartman lifted Jake into his Model A and I held his head in my lap. We drove fast and reckless to the hospital where nurses took him inside.

They washed his face and did things nurses and doctors do. All the time I held his greasy old hat that fell off in the pens. Quickly they rolled Jake into a room so we waited outside until someone could tell us what happened to our old friend.

After a while a doctor came out where everybody was standing around against the walls, and he asked, "Are any of you family?"

Everyone was quick to say no. Jake didn't have any family we could think of. The doctor's question told us that something pretty bad was happening inside the clean white room where they took Jake.

He said, "Jake had a heart attack and things look pretty bad for him." That was the first time I ever saw a heart attack happen. We felt bad about it and I was scared, waiting for the doctor to come back with more news.

When he returned he whispered to Mr. Hartman so low I couldn't hear much of what he said. Mostly he was asking questions. "Do any of you know what his name is other than Jake?"

No one could remember him being called anything else, and none knew of any family or where he came from. Jake wasn't one to talk a lot. At last the doctor said loud enough for all of us to hear, "Well, boys, Jake just died in there, and I'm gonna tell you something you may find hard to believe. Jake is a woman!"

Uncle Billy, who had lived in the same bunkhouse with him or her for a couple of years, couldn't believe it.

"Doc, are you sure about that?"

"I'm sure. I've been a doctor all my life and I can tell you Jake is and always has been a woman!"

The boys at the hospital got pretty quiet trying to figure what they should do. They agreed that since Jake had always lived the life of a cowboy, he should be buried as a cowboy. There was no reason to try to set the record straight now. All agreed, so they shook hands on it, then passed his old hat and collected some money to add to the six dollars Jake had in his pocket when he died.

Back at the auction Mr. Britton announced that Jake was dead, so they passed his hat around some more so the ranchers who had money could help, and then left it at the window where those who sold livestock got paid, and each one chipped in when they collected for livestock sold that day.

There was enough to bury Jake and buy a stone marker. Since no one knew when he was born, they carved the date of his death and the name JAKE. That didn't seem to be enough, and they didn't dare tell what they knew, so they settled on the words, "JAKE WAS A GOOD COW HAND." They laid him to rest wearing clean work clothes and his only pair of boots.

Because I was just a little kid no one shook my hand. Even so, I never told, but they are all dead now, so maybe it is OK. You can't always tell a man, and I thought you would want to know.

SNIP

Every kid needs to own a horse at some time. Snip was my first horse, a rather elderly horse when we met. He was tall, dignified, with a white blaze on his forehead, a long black mane and tail. Over all he was generally red-brown, which Mr. Hartman said was called sorrel.

Snip looked much taller than he really was because I couldn't see over his back. I was a little boy in those days, and everything in my world was oversized. Never having the experience of being any bigger, I naturally thought the world was made with huge spoons that filled your mouth with each bite, chairs too tall for my short legs, door knobs that struck me at eye level, and steps so high I often used my hands to help me climb.

Snip was a too tall horse for a too small boy. I could not saddle him or swing up on his back like Ross and Verl did. I had my ways though. I'd coax him to the corral gate with maize heads while I climbed up on the planks high enough to jump to his broad back. I'd wrap his flowing mane around both my hands so as not to fall off.

At first Snip hardly noticed when I was sitting on his back, but when I shouted and used my heels to get his atten-

tion, he walked slowly along the fence to the water trough, and around and around inside the corrals. As days went by I grew confident enough to open the gate and ride him around the trap and water lot. He walked slowly away from the corrals, and together we explored mesquite trees that grew so close together that the branches nearly drug me off his back. I soon learned to hug his neck so even the lowest branches didn't scrape me off.

Snip had another trick that I learned to handle. He would enter a gate so close to the post that he would mash my leg as he went by. I learned to lift my foot to his back and let him leave horsehair on every gatepost we passed if that was what he wanted to do.

Riding without saddle or bridle was not easy because those trappings are used to guide a horse or stay securely on your mount. As we got to know each other he learned to go where I wanted him to by a gentle pat on the side of his neck or a little kick with a bare foot.

As we went away from the barn, we began to understand each other better. At first Snip walked slowly, pausing to eat. While his head was down nibbling the grass, his mane pulled me forward until I finally had the nerve to let go. Sometimes it seemed he forgot I was up there, at least, while he ate. I'd lay flat on my back looking up at clouds drifting overhead, listening to sounds of birds, crickets, frogs, and windmills, pumping gyp-water. Those days nothing was more important than being friends with my horse.

I learned to scold him to make him pass tempting grass or an ear of corn fallen from a wagon. If I made enough noise and used my heels, he would lope and I loved the feeling of a horse under me as we moved along like we were grown together. At last we changed his gait from a lope to a gallop, and I enjoyed the wind in my face as we raced over pastures together.

Somewhere between a gallop and a walk there was an impossible movement when every hoof hit the ground at a different time. It jarred my teeth loose and made my eyeballs dance! I never liked that motion. However, Snip was one of the best playmates a little boy ever had.

When we were far from the ranch headquarters and it was time to head home, Snip wanted to return as quickly as he could, first loping, then galloping, and at last in a dead run if I didn't hold him back at a steady pace. It was times like that when I learned to talk to him in a voice of authority, not having saddle or bridle or quirt. It takes some tough determination to reason with a horse when you are not yet old enough to go to school.

No matter how I tried, the last quarter of a mile back to the barn would be a horse race, and then Snip would pull one of his nasty tricks, running to the corral gate with me shouting, "Whoa, whoa, whoa!"

Snip wouldn't whoa until he was smack against the gate, and then he would stop — all at once! If I wasn't ready for it, I tumbled over his head either onto the wooden gate or if his nose happened to be over the top, I sailed over it into the corral, landing in a sorry heap.

Owning a horse wasn't easy because somehow the horse thought he owned me. It was my job to feed him. Once I made him sick because I thought I would give him a treat by serving two buckets of feed when he was only supposed to eat one. Horses will eat too much of something they like and get sick, just like little boys sometimes do.

I found out horses in dry lots like green grass. Snip came to me when I brought grass to the corral. He would nibble from my hand, careful not to bite my fingers.

Friends trust each other, but sometimes accidents happen. The big old Cross Ell barn had four huge grain rooms. I'd bring maize heads to feed Snip when I came to visit. One day I held one out and when he reached to eat it, I pulled it closer to me so I could rub his nose. It was out of his reach, so he took one step closer and stepped right on top of my bare foot with his iron horse shoe. It hurt so bad I dropped my maize. Snip picked it up and kept standing on my foot while he ate it. I shouted and beat on his chest with my fists, but he took what seemed a long, long time to eat his treat before he lifted that heavy hoof off my bruised foot.

Snip taught me how to be careful and never to tease animals. It's good to have respect for your animal friends, whether a huge horse or a kitty-cat, or even a baby sister. Sometimes people forget to feed their pets or shelter them from rain or break ice off their water. Snip reminded me to be kind to him, and if I forgot, he let me know with a whinny. He used it to tell me "howdy" when I came to see him, and he had a special way to say, "Let's go play together." Animals are smarter than you think, and if you get to know your pets, they speak in their special way, and if you pay attention, you can respond to them and they understand. The best language is kindness.

Did I really own Snip, or did he just have a trained little boy? Not that it matters. We learned from each other, and maybe that is why every kid needs a horse sometime during his life. Not only does it make you feel big, but the horse can teach some important lessons he can use the rest of his life. Riding Snip I learned to think "horse thoughts."

Together, we had a good time riding around the ranch, only it was me doing the riding and Snip with his feet on the ground. That's something else I learned. Sometimes we forget the difference between who is riding and who is carrying the load.

OLD SETTLERS' REUNION

When the Texas and Pacific Railroad was built, land was sold to settlers so they would generate traffic along the route as they came west to make homes. Every year the old settlers had a big event they called the Reunion.

People came together to tell stories, visit, see how much the younguns had grown since the last Reunion, hear fiddling contests, drink pink lemonade made in wooden barrels, and eat barbecue, beans, and son-of-a-gun-stew. That was the stew that used up of all the innards of the animal — heart, lungs, kidneys, guts, and anything else they happened to come across while butchering steers.

At one reunion I heard a story about the Indian raid in 1878. I listened to stories of the Civil War told by old men who fought at Shiloh and Bull Run. There were younger men from the Spanish American War and a drum and bugle corps made up of veterans of the A.E.F. from the World War of 1918. These events took place under huge cottonwoods trees growing in a low spot beside the railroad. In later years when the town had grown, it moved to the new city park, south of town.

The kids played, ran, and ate until they gave out, then their parents sent them to the wagons to take a nap on homemade quilts. When they woke up there was still plenty to do. One time there was a man who trained a goat and two pigs to do tricks. They could climb a ladder and walk a pair of tight wires and some other tricks I didn't get to see because some pretty girls came along and the big boys went off to talk to them, and we little ones followed to listen to what they said. One can learn by just listening.

If little kids sat quietly and didn't move or ask questions, the old folks would talk to each other and pretend the kids weren't there. Men sat around chewing tobacco, spitting on the ground, and talking about whatever they thought was important. Everyone had sharp pocket knives and cottonwood sticks to whittle, all standard equipment.

These events didn't just happen. They had a special way to begin and everyone followed the accepted routine. It was just like going to church and first singing some songs and praying and making announcements before the preacher started his sermon.

First, one man would reach into the bib front pocket of his overalls and fish out a plug of tobacco. Then he'd get out a well-sharpened pocket knife and cut off a chew. He would offer the plug to anyone who happened to be near by. One by one they cut chews of tobacco, each with his own knife. They sat down one after another finding a place to spit where it didn't bother anyone else. Next they fished around in their pockets where they kept a watch, change purse, and a whetstone, until they could separate the stone from those other pocket treasures.

The tobacco didn't dull the blade, but no one wanted to have a dull knife in his pocket, so they would spit on the stone and begin to rub the blade on it to make it sharper and sharper, until they could shave hair off their arm.

When it was keen as spit and stone could make it, they crossed their legs so they could finish the process on boot leather. Everyone had a special place on the boot where the leather was shiny and worn like a razor strap. This was for finishing the edge on their knife.

Well, with a sharp knife, one just had to have something to try it on, and so the whittling began. Any piece of wood would serve as a whittling stick. Folks could tell time by the stack of shavings on the ground. The longer the whittling, the deeper the shavings. On the courthouse corner there was a big Chinese elm called the Spit and Whittle Tree because that's where men met to do their spitting and whittling. The shavings covered the ground under that tree. Men sat on the corner, facing north or east depending on whether they preferred looking at Main Street or Third Street, and also depending on where the sun was shining at the moment. That's where the sidewalk preachers came to shout their sermons and where news and gossip was traded.

This one time at the Settlers Reunion, the men had eaten barbecue and beans and drunk pink lemonade, and they were ready to take it easy in the shade under cottonwoods. The tobacco was tucked into their cheeks, and the whittling was just beginning to litter the ground with fresh white shavings when the subject of Indian raids came up.

These things are not announced. They just creep into the general discussion and sort of take over, and one by one each man tells his favorite story on the subject.

The county clerk was wearing a black suit and tie with a white shirt, high top shoes, and a city hat without the broad brim. He told about a will he had in the courthouse. It was the last will and testament of a man who was killed in an Indian raid in 1880.

It seems that a man and his son came out on the railroad from back east. They were taking up land, hoping to have a house and a well finished before cold weather so they could send for the mother and daughters.

Word came from railroad people that the Mescalero Apaches had been raiding ranches out west and they needed men to go out there and send them back to the reservation over in New Mexico.

This fellow was civic-minded, seeing it as his duty to go along with his son to lend a hand in dealing with those Apaches. He was a careful husband and father, so he went to a lawyer and drew up a will before he boarded the train to take him 150 miles out west into the Pecos country. It was a good thing he did, because he and his son were killed at a place called Panther Springs.

The clerk remembered reading the will in the public records. This pioneer and his son left all they had to the mother — a section of land, a half built dug-out house, a team and wagon, and a few tools. They had a little cash and some personal things. That was all that was mentioned in the will. He thought that was not much to show for a lifetime spent in this world.

Everyone wondered what became of the wife back east, and did they get the Indians back on the reservation. Those are things that don't go into the record, so the men sat around and whittled and spit and speculated about the worth of life. Could the widow have come out and worked the land? Did she marry again? Where did they bury the man and his son? All these were unanswered questions.

A man named Mr. Crow took over and remembered his grandmother had a run-in with a bunch of Comanches at her place in the Hill Country south of San Angelo. It was in a two-story house made of native limestone with windows fitted with iron shutters that could be bolted from the inside for protection.

Everyone called her Mother Linn. She was left at the ranch with a daughter, daughter-in-law, and five or six kids and a baby. The men had gone to work about two hours ride from the home place, so the women were alone that day.

About mid-morning eleven Comanches came out of the woods and cautiously approached the house as they figured out how many people were there and where the men might be. One of the kids came in yelling "Indians, Indians!" and Mother Linn went outside to size things up.

The Indians drew back into a group as she gathered children from the yard where they were playing and shoved them inside the stone house, like a mother hen hovering her brood. From the doorway she directed her defenses. The only dog left at the house was one nursing a litter of pups. This old dog was not usually as fierce as the hounds that had gone out with the men that morning.

Mother Linn made do with what she had and sicked her bitch on the Indians. Maybe it was because she was defending her pups, but that dog took out after the invaders with a will and would have done them harm, only they killed her before she had a chance.

When the family saw that, they knew they were in for trouble, so they closed the door and got the shotgun and an old rifle and all the ammunition they could gather.

The Indians observed there were no men on the ranch, so they took their time in sacking it. First they killed the hogs and gathered the chickens. The horses and cows were turned out and most of the saddles and wagons were with the men, so there was not much for them to steal. Mother Linn opened the door and set a jug of buttermilk outside. The Indians found it and drank it all. Next she got a crock and filled it with flower, lard, milk, and sugar. She stirred it well, then went to her locked cabinet of ranch remedies where she got some strychnine, the most deadly poison on the ranch.

Calmly she blended the entire bottle of poison into the batter, and then without cooking it she set it outside. The Comanches found it and with two fingers they dipped in and tasted the sweet mixture. In a short time they were licking the bowl, and when there was nothing left they smashed it!

The poison took its toll. One Indian went to the well where he drank water and lay down and died. The others ran off toward the creek, and when the men returned that evening they found five more bodies and no sign of hostile Indians.

"Now that was a story!" Uncle Dee Davis said.

He was a lean, old pioneer who still looked like a cowboy, even at an advanced age. He wore the usual cowboy boots, big hat, tight trousers, and blue shirt, open at the neck. His face was clean shaven and lined with wrinkles brought there by living a lot of years in the weather and wind. No one knew whose uncle he was — he was sort of uncle to everybody who knew him. There was no doubt that he was a real pioneer though. He knew everything about the early days and could recite poetry while telling his stories. He was one of the best, so everyone took a fresh interest in their whittling and settled in to hear the best story of the afternoon. Uncle Dee usually waited to be last, and his story often topped them all.

Uncle Dee moved over to a wagon tongue and sat down so he would be a little higher than those squatting on their boot heels or sitting flat in the dirt. That way he could see all the faces and read their reactions. He used eye contact to make his stories better and draw it out or cut it short to fit the mood of his audience.

He spit out his plug of tobacco so as to have full use of his voice, and he lowered his tone just a little bit at the beginning so everyone would quiet down and lean forward to catch every word.

"Boys, you know me. I was raised here on these plains. I made my own way since I was a kid. It was when I was just starting out when I teamed up with an old mustanger named Mose. You younguns may not know what a mustanger is, so I'll tell you," he explained.

"In the early days there was lots of wild horses running free on the open prairie, and they were called mustangs. Folks who were smart enough to catch them could go out there and bring back lots of horses. They got young cowboys to break them to ride. Once they were gentled down, they could sell them for a good profit. Such men were called mustangers."

Uncle Dee continued his story. "I made a trade with Mose to go round up a bunch of them mustangs and bring them back to the railroad corrals and when we got them gentled up, sell them and split the profit. Mose would buy the grub, furnish our horses and stuff, and we would subtract that cost before we split anything. I had nothing to start with, so I figured anything I made would be all to the good."

By now everybody was whittling in earnest and spitting quiet-like so as to not miss a word. He continued, "We rode out west of the sand hills by where Monahans is nowdays, until we came upon horse tracks. None of them had shoes on, so they either had to be mustangs running free on the range or Indian ponies. Mose followed them a ways and when he didn't see any Indian signs, he came to the conclusion that they were mustangs right enough.

"Once it was clear what we were following, Mose had us settle in to a steady pace, not stopping to rest unless we had to. The ponies were taking their time drifting toward the mountains over in New Mexico, so in a few days we came upon the herd. They were a long way off, but we could count fifteen or twenty horses and mares with several colts.

"We moved in closer until they spotted us, and then the horse race was on! They took off in a stampede, but we didn't try to catch up with them all at once. We just kept our distance and let them run, always keeping them in sight. First Mose would trail them and I'd rest with our spare horses, and then they would circle and I'd cut across and take up following them while Mose and his horses rested. We kept this up for several days, always keeping the mustangs on the move, and never letting them scatter out too much or take time to rest.

"The idea was to tire them out and then close in to where we could get a lasso on some of them. It was all a matter of patience. All the time we were working our way nearer the mountains over there near where Carlsbad is now."

At this point Uncle Dee brought some of the whittlers and spitters into the chase by asking the question, "You all know how it is over there at the edge of them mountains, where the canyons run up into the hill, don't you?"

They all nodded their heads and said they sure did know about the canyons across the state line. When he had them thinking about the lay of the land he continued, "Well sir, there is one place where it's a box canyon with no outlet. If I could drive them horses up in there Mose and I could catch them all!

"That's when my luck ran out! I was so busy trailing the horses, I plum forgot to look out for trouble, and before I knew it, a war party of seven Indian braves was riding down on me. Mose came to join me from about three miles away, and when he cut across toward me, they shot his horse from under him. When they came up to where he was on foot, they killed him, right before my eyes!

"It was right then that I knew I was in bad trouble. I let the mustangs go their own way, and I headed for that box canyon, thinking that I could defend myself from the rocks with only one way in a lot easier than I could outrun them in the open.

"Boys, I want to tell you I was in a fix. My rifle was with Mose and the pack horse, so all I had with me was my Colt six-shooter and there were seven of them. I had to make every shot count, and I was still one cartridge short.

"Those varmints came after me, all confident that they had every advantage, so I headed up the canyon and around one or two bends before I stopped. They would most likely be careful at first, but as they came creeping up, I could get in my best shots."

He took off his hat and wiped his forehead with a handkerchief before going on. Whittling had slowed to a standstill, and no one even bent over to spit tobacco juice now.

Uncle Dee had everyone's undivided attention. "I let them come creeping up the canyon because, by now, they had got off the horses and were closing in on me. I just waited.

"They came closer and closer, so close I could smell them and see the sweat on their faces. They were so close I couldn't miss. That was my only chance. I fired at point blank range right into the chest of the first and second ones nearest to me, as near as from you to me.

"That was two clean kills, and it made them mad as wildcats. They fell back and then came creeping back to get the two dead ones when I shot two more in the head. Four out of seven was not bad when it comes to evening the odds. I was beginning to feel like I had a chance, because surely with four of them dead, they would be scared off and leave me alone long enough to save myself.

"That's where I figured wrong, though. They took cover, and it was still three to one in the fight. They didn't know I just had two bullets left, and I was thankful for that. I was pretty confident I was going to make it, looking at those four dead ones, each drilled with a single shot, so I took my time to get off one more." The old man squinted one eye like he was taking aim, and no one dared to even breathe.

"I squeezed on the trigger, and the dang thing exploded in my hand! I saw I had hit the Indian, but my hand was a mess, and my gun useless. The others came screaming in at me, hungry for the kill!"

No one dared to breathe. All listeners sat frozen in time and space waiting, waiting. I could stand it no longer, "What happened, Uncle Dee?"

"Why son, they killed me!"

Everyone burst into laughter. Whittlers dropped their

sticks, folded their knives back into their pockets, and began to round up their wives and kids for home.

Why, oh why, did I have to be the one who asked?

A GIFT FROM MISS ANTLEY

Mama packed my lunch in a brown paper bag and Daddy gave me a nickel to buy a Big Chief tablet marked with lines and a new penny cedar pencil with an eraser on one end and the other end cut off flat with no point. We were off to town for my first day in school.

There were more children than I had ever seen at one time in my six years of life, and they all seemed to be looking at me in my button-front coveralls and scuffed cowboy boots.

Suddenly Daddy was gone and I was left with a beautiful lady who said, "My name is Miss Antley."

I had never been introduced to anyone like her before and all I could do was stammer, in a weak and frightened voice, "I, I'm, uh, I'm from the Cross Ell Ranch."

Miss Antley asked me my name, and from then on she called me by it. She led me to a desk and said I could sit there every day. It was small, like me, with a seat that folded up. The sloping wooden top had writing scratched into it and a curious round hole for an ink well and a special groove where I could lay my pencil.

With so much to see, I didn't listen to what Miss Antley was saying from her big desk in front of the class. It was my experience that adults seldom talked to children except when they wanted us to stop doing something that bothered them.

Miss Antley was talking and talking before I realized she was calling my name. In a kind and gentle voice she invited me to come to her desk and she treated me like a real person. She gave me a book with pictures of a boy, a girl, a dog, and a cat.

"This is your Bob and Nancy reader. You may take it home with you and bring it back tomorrow," she said.

What a wonderful surprise, a book with pictures and writing to take home to the ranch!

A bell rang and we went out to recess. There were big girls with scrubbed faces and braided hair and rough boys who wore shoes and caps. When the bell rang again, everyone lined up and marched inside where Miss Antley was writing letters on the blackboard. It was there that I started to learn what each one was called.

Miss Antley showed us how the letters go together to make words, and then how the words fit together to tell stories, like those in our reader. I learned every word in our book.

On the road back to the ranch I saw signs with words, Clabber Girl Baking Powder, Bright and Early Coffee, Brown's Mule Chewing Tobacco, El Paso 328 Miles. In the newspaper there were words that told things like "Lindy Flies the Atlantic" and "Stock Market Crashes."

I wondered, "What is a stock market? Do they sell cattle there? And how can it crash?" Miss Antley explained it to me.

She explained words I learned in Sunday school, too. We sang a song about "low in the gravy lay" and she showed me it should be "in the grave he lay." "Bringing in the sheets" was really bringing in the sheaves of grain, and there is no one named Round John Virgin in the song "Silent Night."

There were other things to read: the comics with Krazy Kat, Maggy and Jiggs, Mutt and Jeff, and Buck Rogers. The first book I read all the way through by myself was about General Sam Houston and the Texas Revolution. Later I had favorite authors: Jack London, O. Henry, James Michener. Then I read the Holy Bible and Shakespeare, and books in Latin and Spanish languages.

Miss Antley's gift was teaching me to read, giving me the key that unlocks all the written words in the world. How could I ever thank her for all it has meant?

I wish I could find her and hold her hand and with a grateful heart say, "Thank you for a lifetime of being able to read, one of the greatest gifts one can enjoy."

MY SOUL TO TAKE

Now I lay me down to sleep,
I pray thee, Lord, my soul to keep.
If I should die before I wake,
I pray thee, Lord, my soul to take.

When I was a little kid on the Cross Ell Ranch, I said that prayer every night before Mama tucked me into my little iron bed. She would kiss me goodnight and leave the room, taking the oil lamp away into the front part of the house. I would lie there in the dark listening to the night sounds, and wonder and wonder.

What is my soul? Where is it? What happens if God takes it away and keeps it? I wanted to change that prayer and just say, "Lord, I don't wanna die, not tonight for sure! Lord, please keep me going. I'm just a little kid way out here on this big old lonesome ranch."

The more I thought about my little child's prayer, the more scared I got. I had dreams about death before I woke up. It made me not want to go to sleep in the first place, just thinking about it.

Years came and went, and I continued to wake up in the mornings day after day. I outgrew the little iron bed and had my own boots and a horse, like a real person, well, like a real ranch person.

I still wondered about the soul part of that prayer. To a child, the soul was something mysterious. As I grew up, it didn't get any clearer in my mind. Some things get easier as one matures, but the wonder about the soul still remains a mystery. I tried to imagine where it might be located. Was it in my head, my heart, my chest? Somehow I had a feeling it was about a foot above my head, floating around like an invisible balloon on an invisible string tied to me somewhere. I even jumped up in the air and clapped my hands over my head, trying to catch it in my fingers to see how it would feel.

Daddy said, "Stop that jumping up and down clapping your hands over your head. It makes me nervous."

Well, it was making me nervous, too, but for a different reason. I couldn't find where I kept this thing, my soul. I never have been able to figure it out, but I know it is somewhere, somewhere personal. What's more, everyone has a soul, only I don't think chickens, cows, and hogs have souls, or so my Sunday school teacher told me. I wonder how she found that out.

I was a little bit sad to think that Snip, my horse, and Pudgy, my dog, didn't have souls. I hoped the teacher was wrong about dogs and horses not having souls. But I was having so much trouble locating my own soul that I didn't wonder too long about my pets' souls.

There are some things that are just too much for little boys to figure out, so I asked Mr. Hartman, the ranch foreman.

"Mr. Hartman, where is my soul?"

He looked me straight in the eye and said, "It's headed straight for Hell if you leave the milk pen calves in with their mamas tonight like you did last night!"

That was not the answer I was looking for. I asked Verl, who was several years older than me, and he said, "It's in your heart, like they say, Heart and Soul."

I felt my chest and the thump, thump, thump inside and somehow that didn't explain away my question.

My friend Luis Perez told me, "It's something the priest prays for that goes to Purgatory and stays there a long time because you have been sinful and bad."

Thunder! I didn't know what my soul was and now Luis had turned up something else I couldn't understand, called Purgatory. I wondered if it might be out near El Paso some place or maybe New York. One question at a time was all I could handle.

Finally I just prayed about it. It seems God alone knows where it is, so maybe He would explain it to me if I asked Him real nice and polite like. I hoped to goodness He didn't answer with a bolt of lightning or a clap of thunder.

Pudgy and I went out behind the woodpile where no one was looking and I knelt down and asked him, "God, Sir, where is my soul?"

He didn't answer, but my little dog licked my face and I just waited and waited. There wasn't any lightning or thunder or anything but a mockingbird singing from the top of the lightning rod.

After a while it came to me. My soul is the real me. It's going on forever.

So I decided, it doesn't matter where it is, so long as it is in God's hands. It really doesn't matter.

THE RIDING CALF

One morning at milking time we found Brownie with a new calf. I didn't rush up to her but squatted down on my heels waiting for her to introduce us. Brownie, a proud mama, nudged the bull calf with her nose until he slowly stood up, first on swaying back legs, then on wobbly front feet.

As he swayed from side to side on four pink hooves, his mama washed his face and brushed the glistening coat into spit-curls using her long gray tongue. Brownie was a Jersey, but her baby was marked like his papa, with a Hereford white face and four white stockings. His coat was dark, almost black.

My breath came out in steam that frosty morning, and I felt that I should make the new baby a warm bed. In the corner where the wooden pen brought shelter from the north wind yet was open to the morning sun, I made a nest of sweet red-top cane and alfalfa. After his breakfast of his mama's first milk, he snuggled down for a morning nap, comfortable, clean, and cozy.

It was not long before he came to me in the mornings for a nibble of cottonseed cake or grains of maize eaten from my hand. As he grew I tried riding him, just as I did with all the milk pen calves. Unlike the others that bucked and pitched, he would allow a certain amount of riding in the cow lot. He was gentle and friendly, this special black bull calf that met me every time I came to the corrals.

As days passed I rode him more and more inside the pens, until the time we went out in the water trap and then to the house and by the barn. At first he went where he wanted to go until I taught him to turn by patting him on the neck and soon he would respond as well as a pony. If you have ridden both cows and horses, you know that horses are easier to sit upon, better padded. But a riding calf is such an oddity that it's worth the discomfort.

When the riding was done, he followed me around the ranch like a pet. We were friends. One day he climbed the front porch steps and just for fun — and because Mama was outside feeding her chickens — I opened the door and Riding Calf walked right in to the living room and lay down on the hearth in front of the fireplace, making himself comfortable.

When Mama came in and caught us, he was curled up like a huge pussy cat taking a nap. She wanted to be angry but couldn't help laughing, and so she let him stay a little while. After that he came in several times and was always a gentleman, never once making a mess. Mama said, "You are just lucky he behaves because it will be up to you to clean up if he forgets his manners."

At night Riding Calf stayed in the corrals with the other calves, but by day he was a special pet. As he grew our rides got longer until in the fall I rode him to the schoolhouse. During classes he waited patiently outside, and at recess the children took turns riding him. He shared their syrup biscuits and drank from the well bucket when the teachers were not watching.

Riding Calf was smart as a dog, quickly learning new tricks. He could shake hands, kneel to say his prayers, roll over and play dead, and with one end of a rope around his neck, take part in skip-rope. I could ride sitting on him backwards, steering with his tail in my hand. The girls laughed and squealed to see us do that one.

As he grew, I began to have ideas about becoming a rodeo clown, "THE BOY FROM THE CROSS ELL RANCH AND HIS RIDING CALF." I could see billboard signs pasted on barns and fences in my imagination. I could spend the summer going to rodeos earning cash money, Riding Calf and I performing between contests, riding in parades and the grand entry, me carrying a flag on a spear with the Cross Ell brand on it. Boys never run out of things to dream about.

One afternoon when I came home I didn't see Riding Calf. When I searched and could not find him, I was told, "We took your riding calf to the freezer locker plant today and he was slaughtered for winter meat, just like the others raised in the milk pen." My idea was grand, but it never worked out.

On a ranch everything has its place and purpose. Milk pen calves always go to the freezer. I had not counted on it applying even to Riding Calf. I just thought he was too special. Life is like that. We each have a fate and no matter what we do along the way, we fulfill our purpose, even though we know some special tricks.

A half Jersey bull would become a major problem on a ranch that produces pure bred Hereford cattle, when you stop to think about it. He was fun while he was growing up, but I never took the trouble to train another riding calf. None of them seemed smart enough, and anyway I never had the time. Calves are born to be eaten.

Mr. Hartman, the Cross Ell foreman, said, "Son, you just trained the wrong animal. If you spent your time on a colt, by now you would have a good horse to ride."

"Never ride a calf, and never eat a horse." That is an important lesson I learned as I cried myself to sleep, lonesome for my friend, Riding Calf.

A WHALE BY RAIL

Verl ran all the way to the house. I thought it was because the hot ground was burning his bare feet, but something more urgent was driving him at full speed up on the porch where Baby Sister and I were seated beside the cistern.

"There's a whale in town!" he announced.

"What's a whale doing out here in West Texas?" I asked. "They live in the ocean way out on the other side of California where they grow oranges."

"No, no, no, it's really truly true. There's a whale over in town. Cross my heart and hope to die!" he shouted, all out of breath.

"Stick a needle in your eye?" I added to his vow.

"Stick two needles in both eyes," he said.

That settled it! Verl was telling the truth, as improbable as it might be. A whale was in town. By what miracle could a whale get way out there on our prairie? He sure didn't swim.

There was indeed a whale on a railroad siding on a flat car, and people could go look at it — for a dime.

Milking time found everybody on the Cross Ell down at the barn to talk it over. Mr. Hartman and Sam Callihan were sitting on the corral fence, and Sally Callihan and Old

Doodler and Mama had on their aprons and straw hats and were standing next to the milk pen, and Ross, Geneva, Leon, and Lillian stood ready with milk buckets, while Verl, Baby Sister, and I sat in the dirt, listening, hoping to hear more about the event, a whale in Big Spring.

Arthur Hartman said, "It's the honest truth. They got a sure enough whale down there in the T&P Rail Yards, and folks are paying a dime to go look at it. True Dunnagin told me so down at the mail box when I met him coming back from town. He seen it himself, paid his money and went and looked it over. It's as long as the whole flat car."

I nearly lost my breath with excitement when Daddy suggested we go to town and take a look on Saturday. I had never seen a whale except in my Sunday school book where it told about Jonah getting swallowed up by one and living in its stomach for three days.

Baby Sister piped up, "What's a whale?"

Poor little thing needed it all explained to her, and I was her big brother so I spent the rest of the week explaining it to her, even when she had forgotten what her question was in the first place. I did such a good job of providing her information on whales that I went beyond what I knew about them myself. I just made up what I was not sure of, and she kept me running on and on about whales with her responses of "uh huh."

That meant I still had at least a part of her attention, and that's enough when you don't have anyone else to talk to. Oh, what a long week of waiting that was.

Saturday came and we went to see the whale. I knew where he was a long time before we got near the depot. I could smell whale all the way from B.O. Jones' Red and White Grocery where we had to park because so many people were there to look him over.

We found a line of people waiting their turn, so we went to the end and got in line, too. Baby Sister said, "Ugh! Something smells bad around here, like an old cow died."

Mama said, "Shush! That's whale smell. That's how you know it's a real honest to goodness whale."

I asked, "Mama, do all whales smell that way?"

She replied with a firm, "Hush!"

At last we paid money and climbed up some wooden steps and walked behind the canvas surrounding the flat car, and there was something that looked like it was made out of the same material as old truck tires but smelled to high heavens. I couldn't tell if it was a whale or a mass of blackish stuff, but there was a whole lot of it.

A man in a sea captain's suit with a white hat and walking cane announced, "Ladies and gentlemen, this is a whale, a leviathan of the deep, brought to you from the Pacific Ocean for your inspection. I point out the huge flukes of the tail…"

We had come in from the wrong end, and I was expecting to see his mouth that swallowed Jonah, and his eyes. I was afraid I couldn't hold my breath long enough to walk my way to the front end for a look.

Half way down the car, they had a stuffed mermaid which we could look at for free since we were already there. It was awful with the head and arms covered with hair and a shiny tail with fish scales, and wrinkled like it was about to fall apart.

Next wonder of wonders was a shrunken human head with its eyelids and mouth sewed shut. We had left the old sea captain at the tail end of the whale, and this new adventure was in charge of a younger man in a sailor suit with a little white sailor hat and tattoos.

"This is another bonus attraction we have here, a shrunken human head taken from wild natives of Borneo," he said.

I dreamed about that head for a long time afterward. If I ever had to go to Borneo, I'd be very, very careful. I didn't want to furnish a little boy head to go on a flat car with a stinky old dead whale.

At last there was the head with a mouth full of teeth that looked like straws. The man said it was baleen, and whales strained food through it because they ate little shrimp as their only diet.

"So how come the whale swallowed Jonah with a mouth full of that stuff, straining out all the big things?" I wondered.

I knew something was wrong because the Sunday school teacher said a whale swallowed Jonah, and this whale couldn't swallow a ground squirrel. I believed Mrs. Douglas, she knows about whales and what they can swallow.

I thought I was going to escape at last, but another man in a navy uniform came along with some ambergris. I didn't want to even look at it, much less touch it.

He announced, "Ambergris is made by whales and it is

highly prized as the material from which exotic perfumes are made. It's worth a fortune to the perfume trade. We have here for you a special offer of a bottle of Exotic Perfume for the small price of fifteen cents a bottle. Take one home as a memento of your adventures with this leviathan of the deep."

Geneva bought a little bottle of Exotic. A girl pinned a paper badge on me that said "I've been to see the whale" and made me promise to wear it to school on Monday. I would have promised anything to get back to the Red and White Grocery and the car.

Monday morning I wore my badge and found most of the kids had one just like it, and the girls reeked of Exotic Perfume. The whale had been to town, way out there in the Big Empty. That's how folks get an education, one dime at a time.

IF I WERE BLIND

Because I was ill, first grade lasted only two months and two weeks. The second grade was better, only I had trouble with reading and numbers. A doctor suggested I have an eye examination. Mama was told that one eye was bad enough to declare me legally blind, but the other had vision so I could see at twenty feet what normal eyes should read at sixty feet. He said, "This boy has the eyes of a seventy-five-year-old man."

So at age seven I was fitted with horn-rimmed glasses. My reading and numbers improved immediately, but my nose got smashed out of shape again and again. West Ward School was the toughest in town, and very few children wore glasses. They called me "Four Eyes."

When they called me that, I smashed them in the nose and they smashed me back. Timid kids didn't use that name on me, and tough ones knew it meant a fight, even if they won.

I fought several times a day until even the bullies learned it was not worth the trouble and gave it up. I had a friend named Edward Fisher who also wore glasses, and together we took on the world. Sometimes it was all we could do to keep from crying after losing badly in a fight, but to shed a tear in public would have meant we lost, so we learned never to cry in spite of the nose bleeds, a lesson learned early in life that served us well in the years that followed. Our bond of friendship endured a lifetime, begun in the dusty West Ward school yard.

Having "bad eyes" gave me something else to think about. I wondered, "What if I went blind?"

On the ranch, I'd close my eyes for maybe an hour to experience what blindness would be like. It was scary. The longer I kept them closed the more things I became aware of. These discoveries opened a world I might never have known with both eyes open.

At first, I just listened. There were two windmills at the ranch house. One was a tin mill and the other wooden. I could tell when they were pumping by the sound each made. The tin mill had the sound of iron as it pumped or moved to face the changing wind.

The old wooden mill made a hollow caloop! caloop! as it turned. When there was no wind, we used a gasoline pump that went bang! bang! bang! wheeze, wheeze, bang! wheeze! With those sounds in my mind I envisioned the mills working, each in its own way.

My eyes still closed I could hear cows walking by, and soon I could count them by the sound of their hoofs. I'd think to myself, "There are ten cows going by," open my eyes and usually there would be eight, ten, or twelve. Not bad for a blind guess.

Teams of mules with their iron shoes and pulling a wagon were easy to identify. Harnessed draft animals walked in rhythm. Iron wagon wheels crunched gravel, and rattling trace chains made a delightful jingle as the driver cracked his whip, shouting "gee!" which is mule talk for "turn right." Sounds of a passing wagon were like painted colors to my closed eyes, sorting the action from a mixture of noise.

I learned the difference between a shotgun, a rifle, or a pistol shot. A large caliber gun made one sound and a small caliber another. I could tell a .22 from a .38 or a .45. Now a .44 and a .45 were so similar that I never was sure which was being fired. One is only one one-hundredth of an inch bigger bore than the other, so that's too close to know with the ears.

There's no forgetting the deadly buzz of a rattlesnake poised to strike, the hum of honeybees near their hive, or wasps defending their nest against a little boy about to knock it down with a shingle.

I could hear Mama cracking eggs, beating cake batter, scratching a kitchen match, scooping a dipper in the water bucket. I knew when a calf had lost its mama and when milk cows were waiting at the corrals. I listened for that dull ring of the first milk in an empty bucket and then the mellowing sound as it filled squirt by squirt.

Animals had their own language — mother hens clucking when they found grain on the ground, and that special sound from boxes of mail-order-chicks at the post office. You don't have to see newborn kittens under the house to know when their mama comes to nurse them. Cats whine at the back door when bacon is frying on the stove. Did you ever listen to bacon fry?

The voice of the fireplace speaks the language of burning mesquite, coal, or wood. A pot-belly stove burns with a roar when a draft sweeps smoke up the chimney. Brush fires make little explosions as thorns crackle and pop. Late at night the fireplace slowly goes to sleep as coals die out, break off, and fall into the ashes.

Time has sounds. Mourning doves croon as the eastern sky changes from black velvet to pink of morning light. Their gentle voices greet a world waking up.

Milk buckets clank to the rhythm of a milkmaid's walk on her way to the barn. Feeding livestock has a sound for each animal. Red-top bundles thrown from the loft, shelled corn drum-rolling into a wooden horse trough, the slop, slop, sloppy noise of swill pouring out for the pigs, mules munching corn, cows licking cottonseed cake from their bunker, pigs banging an automatic feeder to shake their rations free, noisy chickens scrambling for spilled grain. Those are morning sounds.

As the day warms, cicada begin a high pitched song in the distance and it sweeps over the ranch as others pick it up like a wave swelling up until it surrounds the listener and then dies away in the distance.

By afternoon the Bob White quail whistles to his mate:

> *"Bob White, Bob White!*
> *Wheat ripe, wheat ripe?"*
> *And the answer comes back,*
> *"Not quite, not quite!"*

That old mockingbird declares his territory from the top of the woodpile, copying songs of other birds. He may position himself atop a lightning rod and get so carried away with his concert that he flies straight up in the air and floats back to his same perch, still singing. Even without eyes, you know where he is and what he is doing.

Guinea hens "pot-track, pot-track" around the yard and warn of any danger with a frightening noise.

As evening falls the whippoorwill calls across the prairie. Bullbats come power-diving out of the sky to scoop up flying termites, mosquitoes, and gnats with a huge gaping mouth and tiny beak.

Darkness falls, gasoline lanterns are lit, with voices like a blow-torch. Washing dishes, sounds of glass and silver bumping together, and Mama's foot treadling her Singer Sewing Machine, clattering the stitches as she mends our clothes. Without looking, I know when she brushes Baby Sister's golden hair, because sparks crackle at every stroke of the brush. If there are tangles, Sister goes "Owooooch!"

Late in the evening Mama plays her upright piano. I can hear Daddy walking across the wooden floor to sit beside her on the bench. They sing together, one of the sweetest sounds of all, "Side By Side," a popular song from the depression days. They're sweethearts as they sing, "We may not have a barrel of money. We may be ragged and funny, but we'll carry on, singing a song, side by side!"

Being tucked into bed has its sounds — a sheet unfolding with a snap and then floating down over a mattress, a pillow being fluffed up, the popping of a polish rag shining shoes for school tomorrow, the lantern leaving the room, its voice becoming faint as it goes away.

The night has dark sounds — coyotes in the brush, a train whistle moans a long lonesome "WoooEuuuWooooA" sound heading west on its way to El Paso. Crickets chirp, pond frogs sing to each other, and at four in the morning a rooster crows, announcing the coming of another day. The Seth Thomas clock on the mantel strikes the hours, tolling time marked by hands on its unseen face.

Even the weather has a voice, a whirlwind rushing past picking up dust and trash in its vacuum as it spins by. Distant thunder foretells a coming storm, raindrops pound on a shingle roof, rattle on a sheet-iron shed, or drum the canvas of my tent. Each has a voice. Hailstones make a fearsome noise hammering tomato plants into the mud. Rusty hinges creak as we slam the door of the storm cellar shut.

Babies crying near the end of a sermon should let the preacher know he has talked long enough.

When you listen, there are pictures in sound all around us, more beautiful than symphonies played by an orchestra on a gilded stage.

If I were blind, I'd still love the world I see with my ears.

REMEMBER THE MAINE

In late summer days, blue skies become contrasts of sunshine and shadow, as white clouds explode like popcorn in the wire basket held close to hot coals in the fireplace. Little clouds become towering thunderheads billowing upward to swell into anvil-tops. Some clouds develop virga, a rain curtain that descends toward earth, not quite reaching the thirsty pastures below. The clouds begin to grumble with distant thunder and soon they arc with bolts of lightning peeking through.

First lightning is hidden inside the cloud, then it streaks out as it explodes. Later it runs across the sky from cloud to cloud until it gets tired and then it strikes the earth with repeated discharges followed by rolling peals of thunder. One can tell how far away it is by counting the seconds between the flash and the sound of thunder.

The virga becomes a solid rain curtain and large drops begin to fall. Soon there is a downpour of a summer thunderstorm. Sometimes the gentle shower grows into a real cloudburst that floods the earth in a matter of minutes. All the meadows become flowing streams, dry ponds become lakes, and frogs wake up from the dry dust of their slumber to croak in chorus letting the world know they are fit as a fiddle and ready for love.

On the Cross Ell Ranch, as the clouds blacken the sky chickens go to roost and the mules bray. My special job was to wait for the rain to wash the dust off the shingle roof and flush the bird nests out of the gutter pipes. When clean water flowed through, it was time for me to climb up on the front porch railing and move the handle on the gutter switch to change the flow of rain water from the front yard into the cisterns, one on the front porch and the other by the kitchen door.

All the water we could catch would be used in the house because the Cross Ell was a dry ranch. Oh, there was water for the livestock, but it was gyp-water, strongly laden with Epsom salts. It tasted good enough, but a few minutes after drinking it one was doubled over with stomach cramps. That is why rainwater was so important. When the cisterns ran out of water, we had to haul it in barrels from the sweet-water windmill on the Coleman Place several miles away. That took all day and required the mules, Babe and Pete, a wagon, and a driver. Those were called "water-haul" days, and little other work was done.

The thunderstorm passed quickly, the sound of it settled to a grumble east of South Mountain Mesa. Water ran everywhere, birds bathed in the puddles, roosters crowed, and livestock moved out to taste the fresh wet grass.

After one of those gully-washing rains my friend Donald came splashing barefoot through the puddles. He was a whole grade ahead of me in school. He knew lots of important things because he read newspapers and could do long division. When I asked him questions he always knew the answers. I looked up to him and liked to go to his house to work his picture puzzle of the United States.

Each state was cut out separately so I learned the shape and where it went in the cardboard frame. When it was completed I could see all forty-eight United States and the waters that surrounded them. He taught me the names. Donald was very smart.

On this particular day we went off splashing in the puddles, with our pants legs rolled up to our knees. We laughed and shouted at the sheer pleasure of feeling the mud ooze up between our toes.

"Oh, Donald, if we only had a boat we could sail it on these puddles."

"Well," he said, "we will just have to build a boat."

First we needed a board that looked like a boat. Soon the boat became a ship in our minds, so we searched for a board that looked like a ship.

On the ranch it wasn't hard to find a good selection of scrap material. The wood pile behind the smokehouse had everything we needed, beginning with a two-by-four about the right length for a model ship. I held it while Donald chopped one end with the axe, making it pointed to form the front of the boat. He said, "This will make it cut through the water. That is the end of the boat they call the bow."

He knew everything!

We found blocks of wood for the superstructure and a piece of broom handle which he carved with his pocket knife to make a mast and crow's nest. We gathered rusty nails and pounded them straight. These would hold the parts together.

We thought we would make a sailing ship, but then Donald said, "This can be a battleship and we will call it the Maine after the one that was blown up in Cuba and started the Spanish-American War!"

I had never heard that story before so Donald told me all about it while we nailed things together. "A battleship has to have cannons and turrets," he explained.

To finish it off he cut small limbs from the lone surviving chinaberry tree and stripped away the bark. After making holes in the ends they looked a little like cannons. We made holes in the turrets and fitted them in, four on the lower and three on the upper. With some string we rigged our ship and it was ready to go to sea.

Now I am sure anyone looking at our work would not have guessed it was a more-or-less scale model of the proud Battleship Maine, either before or after the explosion, but to two little boys it was a work of art. What was not evident to the eyes was created in imagination so the weathered boards became the battleship gray of the Maine.

We took it to the nearest puddle. After a proper launching speech we plopped it into the water. It sailed right side up and was a noble ship indeed, the pride of the Cross Ell Navy.

First we sailed it on the nearest puddle, but it ran aground, so we searched out larger bodies of water, down through the corrals and into the calf trap and beyond into the draw. The draw was the lowest place on the ranch and water flowed into it from the corrals, pastures, and fields until it became quite swift and deeper than where we had rolled our pants legs, and before long we were sailing our ship into waste deep water.

We followed the voyage of the Maine from the safety of higher ground as it floated out of reach into a roaring cataract surging through mesquite thickets and sunflower stalks. By then we were far from the barn, out across the north pasture until we came to the fence where the highway to El Paso went past the ranch.

"Donald, the Maine is sailing out of the ranch!" I cried.

"Remember the Maine!" he shouted.

Right then the ship passed over the top of the north barbed wire fence and shot under the bridge below the highway. We both stood there watching it sail out of sight. I wanted to cry, but Donald was a big boy, and big boys don't cry.

We shouted our war cry — "Remember the Maine!" — several more times until it passed from our view into the Creighton Ranch. We turned and waded back toward the barn and speculated on where our ship might sail.

"It will go on across the Creighton Place and down to the Sulfur Draw by the Texas and Pacific Railroad," I told Donald. I wanted to show that I knew some things without having to ask questions.

Where will it go from there, we wondered. Back at the corrals, it was milking time, so we asked Mr. Callihan about where our boat might go. He explained that the Sulfur Draw ran into the Colorado River and from there it went all the way to the Gulf of Mexico.

We helped carry buckets of fresh milk back to the house. Mama rewarded us with butter spread on bread all sprinkled with sugar. Donald and I sat on the front porch watching flashes of lightning from beyond the sound of the thunder — far past the mesa on the east side of the ranch. It was raining in the next county by now. Stars began to twinkle in the sky, while bullbats made their diving sound as they feasted on mosquitoes and flying termites, and the two windmills sounded off in the fresh evening breeze.

As I licked the sugar off my fingers I asked, "Do you think our little ship will go all the way to the Gulf of Mexico?"

He said, "I don't know, but it really could, because Mr. Callihan knows where the water flows."

Then as we lay back on the porch steps looking into the darkening sky as it filled with stars shining, sewn from endless space, I started laughing at a funny thought,

"Donald, wouldn't it be swell if our little ship sailed off into the Gulf of Mexico and on to Cuba like your map puzzle shows it? It could sail right into Havana Harbor just like the real Battleship Maine? I don't think the chinaberry cannons would scare anyone very much, and I doubt that they would waste a torpedo on the second Maine."

Don exclaimed, "Haw! That would be good, if our Maine sailed right into Havana Harbor, and you know it really could, it really truly could do just that!"

When you are a certain age, you know in your heart that anything could happen, and years later you still hope that maybe it did.

REMEMBER THE MAINE!

DOCK SWAP

I was in the horse corrals by the big barn when he came through the water lot in his big black hearse. It was Dock Swap, the "Trading Man," bumping along through the chug holes stirring up a frightful cloud of dust. A crate of chickens was tied to the top, and inside the hearse were racks of dresses, coats, jackets, and sweaters. Mostly they were second-hand, but some were new, with tags sticking on them. On the fenders were crates and bundles of interesting things; inside, all available space was stuffed with things to trade or sell, depending on whether people had produce or cash money.

As soon as he stopped, I was right there to see him open the door. Verl and Ross came running from somewhere, followed by Mr. Hartman and his wife, Old Doodler, and then Mama and Baby Sister, all anxious to see the "Trading Man." He whipped out a bright red silk ribbon for Baby Sister's golden hair, and Mama tied it in place with a bow. He gave Verl and Ross each a pocket comb, and Mr. Hartman received a whetstone to sharpen his pocket knife. The stone was small and it came wrapped in oil paper so it would stay clean in the front bib pocket of his blue overalls. Dock Swap handed Mama a real palm leaf fan and politely asked if there were other people living on the Cross Ell Ranch that he could present with presents.

We called off their names — Sam and Sally Callihan, Geneva, Lillian, and Leon, Snooky and Irene, his mama. Daddy and Charlie, Snooky's daddy, were in town.

Before throwing open the double back doors of the hearse, he gave us time to round up the missing folks. It didn't take long with the excitement that comes with a visit from Dock Swap and his rolling storehouse of surprises.

Right off Mama said, "I don't know why you bother to stop here. The depression is so bad none of us have any cash money to buy anything these days."

Dock smiled a broad grin. "Madam, (that sounded respectful and dignified when he said it) you don't need money to trade with Dock Swap. I see enough red hens in this very barnyard to buy you anything you desire. Do you by chance have any fresh country eggs, butter, sweet cream, or produce from your garden? It's all as good as cash."

We had everything he mentioned and, besides that, there was a ham in the smokehouse and some lard in a bucket, a rawhide on the corral fence, and fox, coon, and rabbit skins collected by the boys on their trap line, and one pelt of a coyote Leon had shot from half a mile away.

Right away I traded my four rabbit pelts for a handful of marbles. Mama had fifteen dozen eggs which Dock placed in a large box tied to the hearse bumper. The box had cardboard egg spacers to keep them from breaking.

From inside the hearse came treasures I had never thought about. Tennis shoes that were hardly worn at all, medicines in colored bottles, healing powders, liniment good for ailments of horses and mules, balm for collar scalds, strains, and cuts.

He had feathers and ribbons to trim a lady's hat, buttons and thread, scissors, creams and lotions, and oil that smelled of bay rum and would make a boy's hair lay flat when it was parted down the middle. There were extracts of vanilla, almonds and lemon, pepper grinders, coffee beans, books with pictures, and bullets to fit any gun. That "Trading Man" had things to tempt every one of us — stick candy for the babies and something to stick down false teeth for the old folks.

When he finally left the ranch he took with him our cured ham, half dozen Rhode Island Red Roosters, a quilt that Mrs. Callihan had pieced together, a lot of rawhide boot strings Verl cut with his knife, and I don't know what else.

In return we had shoe polish in black, brown, and a purple color called ox-blood, snuff, tobacco, medicines and extracts, some clothes, and a lot of things we didn't know we needed when his hearse rumbled over the cattle guard.

Way out there on the range we didn't get many visitors, so Dock Swap was a special sort of man. Wherever he went he traded for what people had. It was not often that any money changed hands. The sweetness of the stick candy in our mouths was no nicer than the memory of the man called Dock Swap. He was our friend, never taking advantage of simple folks. When trading was all done you could count on him to throw in something extra. The Mexicans call that *pelon*, usually a special brown sugar candy. He was like that.

Another thing, before he started to show you what he had to trade, he first gave out presents to everyone, and while he did that he would make us laugh. That day he asked a riddle.

"Sirs, do you any of you know what a jaybird can do that no other animal in the whole world can do?" he asked us.

No one knew though we guessed several things. Finally he asked, "Do you give up?"

We gave up one by one.

"The one thing a jaybird can do that no other creature on earth can do is HAVE BABY JAYBIRDS!"

He had us there!

I figured the things we traded to him were sold in some town or traded to people on ranches along his way. He knew more news than the *Fort Worth Star-Telegram*, news about the neighboring ranches and faraway places. He knew good news about newborn babies and cotton that made a bale to the acre. He knew bad news about who got caught making bootleg whiskey and was now in the county jail and who got injured when a mule kicked him in the head. We kept him on the front porch sitting in the shade and talking by feeding him mother's molasses and pecan pie and drinking Old Doodler's never-empty-coffee-pot brew.

That was Dock Swap, who told us all about everything. One time he didn't come back anymore, and we missed him. I wonder if he had a real name, or a little boy like me, or a home someplace, or did he always stay with his big old black hearse full of clothes and chickens.

MEMORABLE EVENTS

I didn't fall off the turnip wagon out there on the Cross Ell Ranch. We had all sorts of advantages, same as big towns like Abilene, Fort Worth, and El Paso. Culture just came along, and we took advantage of it at every opportunity.

The Don Cossack Chorus came all the way from Russia to sing at the City Auditorium, and the Vienna Boy's Choir. Ringling Brothers Barnum and Bailey Circus came one time, and the elephants mashed round holes in the hot asphalt pavement with their big feet, and though the mayor and city council wanted the circus to pay damages, they never did.

The Army camped near the ranch when they were going from Fort Bliss to Fort Sam Houston. Moving picture stars came to the Lyric and the Queen theaters, and Thurston the Great sawed a lady in half and then put her back together again at the Ritz Picture Show. Admiral Byrd landed his Ford Trimotor Airplane and took folks for a flight around town for five dollars each so he could have money to go back to the South Pole. Amelia Earhart landed her Autogiro for gas one time.

Churches had lectures by missionaries from Africa who told how bad it was over there where people didn't have electricity and running water. They asked for money to improve life in Africa. I hoped some day the Africans would help us get drinking water on the Cross Ell. If we could find it, I know Mr. Hartman and Sam Callihan could pipe it into the kitchen.

Once or twice a year the medicine shows came to town. One was called the Tate-Lax show, and you recognized it by the trailers lined up with the outsides covered with slabs of bark sawed off a single giant California Red Wood Tree. Lined up trunk-to-tail they looked like a huge redwood lying on its side. They played banjos, sang songs, and sold Tate-Lax, which helped people with sluggish bowels.

The Harley Sadler tent show sold saltwater taffy in a box with "a prize in each and every package" before a show started. The stage was filled with prizes, and people came forward to exchange prize tickets for blankets, dishes, and cash. The only thing I ever got was a hair net.

It was announced, "There are three diamond rings hidden in these boxes of candy, and tonight three of you lucky people will go home with genuine diamond rings."

A girl found a ticket in her box and ran down the aisle to the stage where a lady in a pink dress presented the ring. I know she got a diamond because I could actually see a diamond in there when I looked close.

At Cunningham and Philips Drug Store there were all sorts of interesting things to witness. The first marvel was when Shine Philips built the first telephone office in town and strung phone lines up and down Main Street. The drug store number was "NUMBER ONE." No one could ever forget their phone number if they had a phone.

Now that's something we had, a telephone, on the Cross Ell Ranch. I never talked on it because by the time I came along the phone was long gone and the line disappeared, but I know it was there because white insulators were nailed on fence posts where it used to be.

A phone office wasn't all they had at the drug store. One month a man removed corns from people's feet and calluses from their hands. He had a sign in the window that said "We are harvesting Howard County's corn crop."

There stuck on the front window were hundreds of corns and the most interesting thing were two footprints which were really calluses removed from someone who had probably gone barefoot all his life.

Then there was the mechanical man in the window. I stood for over an hour trying to figure out if he was real or just a machine that looked like a man. I waited and waited for him to blink his eye but he closed them slowly ever so often and when he opened them he looked right through me at nothing in particular. His movements lurched like wheels, and wires moved him from inside his peppermint-striped jacket. I know he was a real man, but I never could be certain.

Baby Sister came with me to look at him, but all she did was tug on my hand and stamp her foot saying, "I want to go home! I want to go home! I want to go home!"

So I took her home.

There was "Big Boy," a longhorn steer, the biggest steer in the world. It cost a dime to see him. Not long after that a man came by with the world's smallest team of mules. They were smaller than bird dogs. He had a little wagon and harness, and he chained a monkey to the jump-seat like he was the driver, only the man held a line to their bits so they would run in a big circle with that monkey looking backwards to see where they had been instead of paying attention to where they were going.

During the depression there were empty store buildings along Main Street, and that's where I saw the Robert Ripley Believe-It-or-Not Museum, across from the Albert M. Fisher department store.

There was a glass blower who made a sailing ship of colored glass and birds with long sharp bills. He made tables and chairs for a doll house. I watched for hours.

There was the world's skinniest man and the man who felt no pain, wearing a safety pin through each ear, and he held his socks up with thumbtacks. I saw a man swallow some swords, sometimes two or three at the same time. He really did swallow them because at the end of the show he swallowed a neon light tube and you could see his throat glow red.

Robert Wardlow, supposedly the world's tallest man, came to the O'Rear's Shoe Store, and they gave away an electric train to the kid who could guess how many pennies it took to fill his huge shoe in the store window. I didn't win, but that was OK because we didn't have any electricity to run it. He was a really big man, over nine feet tall if I remember right. He died young. Being tall was bad for his health.

A skating rink came along every year and stayed for months. It was under a tent with a floor so smooth you didn't realize it came apart and was hauled around West Texas from one town to another. When high winds came along they dropped the tent and snubbed it down to protect the flooring until things calmed, then skating went on as usual.

How we could skate. I loved doubles where I could ask any pretty girl without a partner if she would skate a set with me. I met ranch and Oil Patch girls that way. The only thing better than skating doubles was skating trios — I could pick out two pretty girls at the same time. If I picked a popular girl I had to share with her some other cowboy. Skating rink music was some of the best ever played — *South*, *Skaters Waltz*, *Indian Summer*. We always skated to music, heard above the roar of wheels on maple flooring, so loud it rang in my ears all the way home.

Rodeos were exotic events in our lives, to the point that some boys and girls made a career of it. Anabell, the high school class beauty, competed in Madison Square Garden in New York City. The Chesterfield cigarette company chose her to be the Chesterfield Girl of the Month and used her picture in national magazines and highway billboards. We used to ride down the highway to see Anabell smiling at us from a sign the size of a railroad boxcar.

An oil well being drilled just east of the Cosden Oil Refinery hit an air pocket. Not any old air pocket. This well drilled into something that blew the tools out of the hole right up through the derrick crown block. Air pressure was so great they could only estimate it, and from time to time stones and rocks of salt came up like cannon balls. It was known as "that air well," and she blew for six or eight months before it could be capped. Oil men lost interest in what else may have been a mile or so below the prairie.

Then there was the convict in the state pen who wrote a musical cantata about Big Spring. It was good enough that the city chorus produced it and everyone came out to hear the music. They got the warden to let him come hear his work. Naturally everyone loved it because it was about us. Such was the approval of the Big Spring cantata that local citizens got him a pardon. Sad to say it didn't make a reformed man of him, and he was soon in trouble and back in the pen.

Between the State National Bank and the Busy Bee Café was a tattoo artist and a shooting gallery with moving ducks and pipe clay targets. Every spring there was a rattlesnake roundup. We had a lot of things which I have forgotten, but it is safe to say we never lacked for exotic events. There was always something going on, and if it wasn't, we started something.

GOOD FENCES

Growing up on the Cross Ell Ranch brought new duties with every birthday. One I hadn't counted on was building fences. Grandpa said, "Good fences make good neighbors."

I should have known there was something to learn from his wise saying, but at that age fence building is one job I would happily forsake. Mr. Hartman, the foreman, considered it one of his duties to instruct me in the art of stringing barbed wire and setting cedar posts, and if the cows could still get through it when I thought I was finished, he could explain in words I understood that it had to be done over, and done right.

Cows give hard examinations, trying to get to the grass that's always greener on the other side of the fence. Cows don't care if boys have to replace a whole section of fence, and they are not the only threat.

Once I built fence on a large sand drift by the maize field. In a few weeks tumbleweeds had blown against the wire, and sand driven by sixty-mile-an-hour winds buried four of the five wires stretched to keep the cows out.

I brought a wagon load of tools, posts and used barbed wire, set new posts beside those buried in the drift and wired them together. I strung six new wires above the top strand on the old fence. I knew the field would be safe from those hungry Hereford cows.

Following several days of dust storms and hard west winds. Mr. Hartman looked me up and said, "Son, them cows is in the maize again!"

"How could that be?" I asked in disbelief.

"Go up there and see for yourself, and take your fence tools with you."

When the cows are in the field, you don't wait for Saturday to see about it. You "light a shuck" and that means you go now, now, now! Stupid cows will eat themselves into the bloat and maybe swell up and die, and it doesn't take long — or they might destroy the crop and a year's work growing it.

I took Snip and went at a gallop to round up the cows and get them out of the field before I could fix that old fence. All the way across the pasture I tried to imagine how they could go over eleven wires, five on the first fence and six on the new top post.

I was not prepared for what I found. They walked UNDER MY FENCE! Days of hard winds had blown sand away from that gosh awful fence I'd built. Ten or fifteen posts were completely suspended in the air held in place by eleven strands of barbed wire. So much sand blew away that cows strolled under the bottom wire.

By lantern light I strung temporary wires on a third row of posts that connected the ridiculous high wire fence to the ground. It was such a tangle that in the morning I hurried back to clean up the mess before anyone else made fun of me as a fence builder. Fences are not something one thinks a lot about. They are like houses, clean sheets on your bed, socks rolled in little matched bundles ready to wear, school buildings, parents. They are always there when you need them. Kids don't consider that these things don't happen by themselves. The sun comes up and the rain falls, it's the hand of God.

It is a sign of growing up to learn the truth: sturdy houses, clean sheets, breakfast on the table, hot coffee on the stove, mothers and fathers are all things that come to you through effort of someone — and the design of a loving God.

Where were Roscoe, Albert, and Sam when I needed help stretching wire, digging holes, and driving staples into wood half as hard as iron? They were looking over me to see that I didn't hang myself in the tangled barbed wire web I strung out there on the prairie all by myself. So why couldn't they keep me from hitting my thumb with the hammer, making blood blisters under the nail? Life gets tough, and we grow tougher as we mature. It's hard building a fence where the ground keeps moving around.

Mr. Hartman arrived to inspect my latest effort, and I got an idea that he was not completely pleased with what he saw, because he took me to another part of the ranch to show me another fence.

"Son, look there at that stretch of fence. It's fine as any you will see. I want you to know it was built by a one-armed man. A ranch with good fences is admired and it speaks well of the folks who lived there."

That was an interesting fence. I had looked at it all my short life, but this was the first time I'd really seen it. Every post was in line, straight as a string and the same height. Sighting down the row, each post was as even as a carpenter's level could make it. Every staple was driven so it didn't bite into the wire. Leaving space to move as heat and cold changed its length. Wires were "singing tight." When wind blows hard the wires on a well-made fence will sing and hum.

Slim stays that didn't touch the ground were wired to the strands between posts. These kept proper spacing so cows couldn't force their way through. Corner posts were braced at right angles and bound with twisted wire to secure them.

"Didja ever see a finer fence anywhere? Looky there how he stripped the cedar bark off them posts and pointed the tops so they don't collect rain water and rot. Now that there is a first rate fence, built by a one-armed man all by himself," Mr. Hartman observed.

That fence was built by a one-armed man? I wonder how he managed the post hole diggers with only one arm, how he stretched each wire exactly the same. How did he hold a staple and hit it with the hammer? Somehow that man worked it out and did an elegant job.

I'd like to find him so he could teach me a thing or two about fence building, but I never had the chance. I didn't even know his name. He had great pride in his work to take such pains on a ranch that he didn't even own.

It was our Cross Ell, so I tried to do better and better as fence work stretched out mile on mile in all directions. Still I couldn't quite match the work of this one-armed guy. I had two arms, so why couldn't I build a fence as good as his?

It made me want to go back and build that maize field fence all over again and do it better. Of course I didn't rush back that day. Cows found weak points, and I got a lot of practice on that stretch of wire before I left the ranch to seek my fortune as an adult.

One day in town I saw another one-armed man selling pencils on the street. Being a kid, I didn't hesitate to ask him, "Mister, how did you lose your arm?"

He said, "It was shot off in the war with the Germans over in France." He went on because he had me as an interested listener.

"That's why I'm handicapped and can't work. That's why I stand on the street corner selling these here pencils."

I thought about him as we went back to the ranch behind the steady gait of our mules, Babe and Pete. I wondered about the man who built the fence. Maybe he lost his arm in the war, but he wasn't selling pencils — he was working with his one good arm. I never met him, yet he is an example that pride in our work doesn't depend on two good arms. It comes from the heart. He may have prayed, "Thank you God for leaving me one good arm. With Your help that's all I need."

The best barbed wire fence I ever saw was built by a one-armed man.

THE WAGON FAMILY

In 1934, the Cross Ell Ranch was having problems. Cotton was a nickel a pound, cattle sold for a dollar a head, and people burned off their cane fields because binder twine to tie the bundles cost more than the bundles would bring.

There was little to be thankful for at Thanksgiving when the Wagon Family came to the ranch house door, with the mama and papa, three kids, and grandpa all living in a rickety wooden covered wagon, drawn by two skinny horses. They asked if they could camp in the north pasture and gather wood and water.

They were welcome to all the mesquite they needed, only they had to grub it out of the ground because there is more root to a mesquite than there is top. Water was another question. We hauled drinking and wash water from the Coleman well two miles south on another part of the Cross Ell. Headquarters wells produced only gyp water, too hard to wash with and it caused awful stomach cramps in people. Only the animals managed to drink it. We caught rain water to cook with and wash hair, in the two cisterns, on the porches.

The Wagon Family offered to haul water for both families and use their team. This was a good exchange, so they camped in the draw all winter. The daddy helped with the cows and mended fences, and we gave them milk, and bundles of red-top cane for their skinny horses.

I asked their kids where they were going, and they said, "We're going to California where we can pick oranges right off the trees, beside the ocean where seals lay on the sand in the sunshine."

That sounded like an adventure, and I secretly wished I was going with them past El Paso, across the desert, over the mountains to sunny California where oranges grow.

The weather turned cold, and one night their mama came to our house to ask if the kids could stay with us because the grandfather was sick. We slept on pallets in front of the fireplace in the living room. At breakfast time, she came to the back door to tell us grandpa died during the night, with something called TB.

Mama gave her one of our bed sheets, and they both went to the Wagon Camp, washed the old man, and sewed him up in the clean white sheet. Cross Ell men buried him east of the big barn, under a cholla cactus with his head facing east, so he would see Jesus on Resurrection Day.

Later that winter the wagon kids spent another night with us when their mama was sick. Next morning they had a baby brother. They were happy, and we went down to see him, but he didn't look like much, not nearly as pretty as a Hereford calf.

At Christmas time we invited the Wagon Family to eat with us. We had one of Mama's turkeys with cornbread stuffing and quail we trapped. The wagon man brought four cot-tontail rabbits. It was a feast! Daddy said a longer blessing than usual before we ate. Afterwards they talked and let us kids listen.

The Wagon Family had come from back East where they starved out on their farm, so they were moving out West to find their fortune in Sunny California under the orange trees beside the ocean. The team was in better shape now, and they thought they could make ten or twelve miles a day. Again I wished I could go along for the adventure.

We talked about things we were thankful for in spite of hard times. There was the new baby, friends to share with, hope of a bright future, and another year to plant a crop. It made us feel good sitting together, counting our blessings, and eating a second piece of sweet potato pie with another glass of milk. The Wagon Family stayed on through a January ice storm, until we had a few warm days in February, and then one morning they were gone. We sent them off with extra feed for the horses, a ham and some bacon and lard from our smokehouse, and flour, sugar, and meal. They head-ed west toward Midland, Pecos, and El Paso, leaving just after milking time on a clear frosty morning. We missed them.

When spring came, I was out by the cholla and it was cov-ered with pink flowers. A cactus wren was building a nest in the spiny branches above the grandpa's grave. I remembered how we shared Christmas when we counted our blessings.

Grandpa is at rest under the cholla until Jesus takes him to Heaven. Those fortunate kids were on their way to

California where orange trees grow. Old people die, leaving room in the wagon for a baby, while grown people make a better life for the children. Flowers bloom on the cholla, Jesus knows the old man is waiting, and the cactus wren is building a home for her family. There are new calves on the range, and it's time to plant again.

THE JONES PLACE

There was a family named Jones, an old man and his wife who lived in a little two-room house part way in to town from the ranch. They must have been in their eighties, yet they managed to scrape out a living with the help of their sixty-year-old retarded son named Junior, and a few head of livestock, a little sandy field, and a mesquite pasture. They had a tumble-down barn and a board-and-wire corral, some chickens and pigs, the usual starvation acres in need of repair.

When we passed by on the way in to town we always waved "howdy" to whomever was sitting on the front porch of their little unpainted house set back about four wagon lengths from the county road. Folks used to stop there to pass the time of day, leave a newspaper, or share a watermelon and see if they were well and able to still manage. The weatherbeaten two-room house had been there longer than anyone could remember — they were just a part of the community.

One clear cold January morning a neighbor named Clyde Dooley was driving his Ford tractor and towing a wagon into town. Mr. Dooley was the first rancher to own a tractor, and as he came down the lane he saw the three Jones people sitting in the dirt beside their mailbox out on the road. They were wrapped in quilts and were still wearing their nightclothes, and were barefooted. Up where the house had been there was only a fire-blackened chimney standing amid the smoking ruins of their little home.

Clyde asked them, "How did the fire start?"

No one could tell him anything. They were cold, frightened and unable to talk about it. Mr. Dooley walked around the burned-up place to take stock of the situation. He gathered the Joneses in the wagon and returned to his place, where Mrs. Dooley fed them breakfast and found clean clothes, shoes, coats, hats, and gloves for all of them. I have no idea where she found everything, and I'll bet the Dooleys were a little short of clothes that winter, but country people are like that, always ready to share with each other. Even after a hot breakfast of grits, coffee, and eggs, they still could not speak.

There was no telephone to call for help, so Mr. Dooley got his two big sons, Rex and Bob, to gather tools, nails, boards, and sheet iron and load it in the wagon. The six of them climbed into Mr. Dooley's wagon and returned to the burned-down house. By now the ashes were cool enough to rake through looking for anything that might have survived the fire. Then Rex and Bob unloaded the wagon supplies, and Mr. Dooley left the Joneses at their place while he drove on in to town.

That morning we were in the old pickup truck when we saw the disaster and the poor Jones family still wrapped in their quilts standing helplessly beside their battered mailbox. Rex told us to look for his father at the lumber yard, so we went on our way. There some boys loaded our truck with lumber and sent us on back to the Jones's. When we drove up there were about thirty people busily going over the ruins. Teams of mules and horses were tied up in the brush; cars and trucks were parked everywhere.

The little old house had been built on stone piers and wooden blocks so it stood off the ground by about three feet. Someone had stacked stones in place and laid out a heavy wooden frame on top to them. One of the boys had a carpenter's level and was giving orders to shim up one stone or another to get the foundation perfectly flat and steady.

Others were raking the ashes out of the way of the builders, sifting through them to see what could be salvaged. The pitiful pile of things included an iron skillet, an axe head, some usable hinges and a pile of burned nails. Two boys were pounding the nails straight on an old tree stump so they could be used again. A black man was carving a new axe handle from a piece of wood.

Soon the floor was laid over the foundation timbers, and the walls were going up. I was small, so I scampered over the roof rafters guiding boards to carpenters waiting to nail each one in place. By accident I reached out and touched the chimney and was surprised to see that it rocked back and forth with my slightest touch! Mr. Dooley saw what I was doing and shouted up to me, "Careful, son, don't shove that chimney over. We're gonna wire it to the house and use it just like it is!"

By bracing the chimney against the rapidly rising house and propping new stones into the foundation, they were able to fasten the house solidly against the trembling chimney until it was secure.

No one stopped for lunch or rest. The work went on without a blueprint or plan. These people knew what to do without direction — each did a job.

By afternoon the house looked just like the one that had been there before the fire, only the lumber was bright and new instead of being gray and weathered to match the outhouse and barn. There was no electricity or plumbing — there never had been on that farm — so it was not missed in this new house. There were two rooms, one for cooking and eating, and another for living and sleeping, just as there had been before. There was a front porch where the family could sit and look out at the county road and see when the postman came by the mailbox, and a front and back door, each with wooden steps leading up from the hard-packed ground that made up the yard.

During all the rebuilding, the three Joneses stood silently to one side holding on to their quilts for security. I don't remember them saying anything all day long. They watched as their neighbors built a new house.

As the sun began to set, we gathered around the well and drank cool fresh water from the bucket, pouring some over our hands and heads to clear away the ashes and sweat. The men were satisfied with the day's work. Two of them had worked under the one shade tree to build a table and three chairs from fresh lumber, and someone had arrived with bed-steads, springs, and mattresses. Someone else nailed shelves in the kitchen part of the house and replaced the wooden mantel over the fireplace.

There was a sweat-stained Stetson hat on the ground beside the well, filled with pennies, dimes, and quarters, and some paper money, too. That was remarkable because in those days, money of any sort was hard to come by. I never owned a dollar bill until I was twelve years old. No one asked where anything came from or who gave what. It just came together as it was needed. No one said what they had put off to come spend the day working at the Jones place. They had changed their plans and done what they could.

In the twilight, a new fire burned in the old fireplace, started from freshly gathered wood, and a new coffee pot boiled its special smell into the evening air along with the promise of supper. At last the Jones family climbed the new steps into their house and spread their quilts on the new beds and sat down to eat the evening meal. But first, they bowed their heads and I could hear the father saying thanks for the blessings of that day and the food on the table.

Teams were untied, wagons rattled off down the road toward homes, pickup trucks grumbled to life, and headlights poked feebly at the gathering darkness as they threaded their way through the mesquite brush back to the road. Light from a new oil lamp gleamed through the opening where tomorrow windows and doors would be installed in the Jones Place. Those were things that had to be put off until another day.

Anything lacking would be made right tomorrow. The fire had taken everything they had, and still they would sleep in a new house that very night. It had been a good day because we liked ourselves better that night, and we loved our neighbors in a special way. We looked after our own no matter what age or color we were.

One of the men said, "It makes me think that when we die, we lose everything, but whatever we lose we are gonna get back, only it'll be all new and better."

No one said much about that day afterward — they didn't have to. The action spoke louder than words.

EVERYTHING DIES OF SOMETHING

My little dog died when a car ran over him. A little rabbit died when a hawk swooped down from the sky and carried him away. The hogs died in the fall when a "blue norther" came whistling in from the panhandle and brought with it what we called "hog killing time" and they became meat in the smokehouse for winter. Then grandmother died with a cancer, and Mrs. Coleman's husband died. I don't know why. Death was no stranger at the Cross Ell Ranch.

Everyone knows death comes to all things. Frost comes and kills the cotton fields in a single night, children die of pneumonia, and mothers died having babies. Chickens died so we could have company for Sunday dinner. There were grave markers out on the prairie where the pioneers met death, and we found graves of Indians who lived before us.

Death always happened to someone else, but the thought that some day I would die bothered me even in those early days. No living thing escaped a final encounter with death. It was scary to think about when people I knew died. I missed them. Folks cried at funerals, and I refused to go if there was any way to avoid it. There were times when I could almost feel death creeping up behind me. A little boy I knew from Sunday school said, "I'm never going to grow up."

His name was Truva Lay and his father was a house painter, and before he ever started to school he died of diphtheria. How did such a little boy know he was never going to grow up?

Once I heard my grandfather who was a doctor tell about an island where they sent people with a dreadful disease called Hansen's Disease or leprosy. He went there to learn about it. His daughter, my aunt, said, "Papa! Aren't you afraid you will catch that awful disease and die from it?"

He answered her, "Daughter, at age 80 I would as soon die of Hansen's Disease as anything else that is going to get me."

He knew he was going to die soon because he was so old, and he was no longer afraid of death. Truva Lay was such a little boy, and he knew and he was not afraid, either. Preachers say no one who is saved should fear death.

As I worked in the fields chopping weeds from the mile-long rows of growing cotton, I had time to think about death and life and living on the ranch. Out there under the endless Texas sky I realized the truth. Everyone dies of something.

I heard grown people say, "Don't put sugar in your coffee, it's bad for you, it'll kill you. Don't be a bronc buster, you'll break your neck and wind up dead. Don't sleep in a draft, you'll catch your death of cold. Don't drink milk when you eat fish, it's poison." People were always forecasting death in one form or another.

At last I figured out one truth, that everybody dies of something and there is absolutely nothing that anybody can do to prevent death overtaking us.

I liked Grandpa's idea, "I would as soon die of Hansen's Disease as anything else." He had no fear of leprosy because he knew the truth and accepted it — we all die of something.

I heard a drinking lawyer say, "Son, there are some folks that are just naturally born to be hung. They can hunt grizzly bears with a switch or drink rot-gut whisky all their lives and it won't kill them because they are living out their life with a hangman's noose at the end, and no matter what else they do they will keep their date on the gallows at the end." I didn't exactly believe all he said, but it had a ring of truth to part of it since alcohol is what killed him.

When I stopped worrying about all the things that might kill me, I started thinking about what came after. In the springtime we planted cottonseed in the Texas earth. I watched them sprout, grow, and bloom in the heat of summer, confident that wind and bugs would spread pollen. Bolls would swell and dry and pop open, turning the field white with cotton, and one day frost would come and kill every last plant. We would pick the cotton and save the seed for next year's cycle of planting.

When the Wagon Family buried the old man beside the cholla cactus in the pasture east of the house, I knew they were only turning under the old dried stalks back to the soil. The seeds of that old man were sprouting in the fields of Heaven in the next season. He wasn't even old any more, but young and tender and beautiful in a way I couldn't understand any more than I can figure out how a cotton plant can grow from that fuzzy seed I planted in the springtime and how the bee will find the flower and how another seed will grow to plant next year's cotton.

I don't have to know how all that takes place. Later on when I went off to war and learned of my schoolmates dying on beaches and in the sky and sea, I could understand enough to not be afraid. After all, everybody dies of something sometime.

But until that something catches up with me, I'm gonna live, live, live!

THE RISING SON
GROCERY STORE

At first, living on the ranch was lonely because there were so few people in the Big Empty. Grandfather sold part of the ranch to build an airport, with a large metal building called an airplane hangar and lights that burned all night. There was one light, a revolving beacon to guide planes to the airport in the dark. Before it came we had lots of coyotes, but the light sweeping the prairie twice a minute must have scared them away because we didn't see many after it came.

When the oil was found east of the ranch, folks called it an Oil Boom. People coming to work on the wells were called Boomers. First just the men came, but before long they brought wives and kids. There weren't any places for them to live so they pitched tents or slept in their cars, and some lived in wooden packing boxes.

Daddy and a partner marked off a town site with sticks and flags and sold lots where people could build homes right out where the oil wells were springing up row on row in all directions. They built houses in a few weeks and moved in. Daddy gave land to build a school and some churches, and soon there was a new little town on the prairie.

His partner, Mr. Stewart, came to the Cross Ell Ranch to talk about their new town. One night while sitting in front of the fireplace Daddy said, "This town needs a name. What will we call it?"

Mr. Stewart said, "Why don't you name it after yourselves, Bruce and Nell? You could call it Brunell."

Daddy had another idea. He suggested, "This oil field has hit four oil sands at four different depths. We should call it Four Sand."

That is what they named it, though later people who opened the post office changed the name to Forsan, Texas. It was an exciting time, and people built other little towns called Otis Chalk, Alward, and Ross City. Some had post offices for a time, but only Forsan survived the Oil Boom days. That was probably because of the school and churches.

Businesses started up — a doctor's office, rooming house, welding shop, and oil refineries where they made gasoline and kerosene from the crude oil. More natural gas was left over than they could sell, so they burned it on top of tall pipes called flares that lit up the prairie for miles around. Oil smelled of rotten eggs — "The smell of money," folks said. People came from everywhere to work in the Oil Boom. Daddy's brother, my Uncle Paul, came all the way from Chile in South America, where he had been working as an engineer in the copper mines. He was a nice uncle, without much hair and with an American flag tattooed on the muscle of his arm. When he made a fist the little flag waved at me. He had a truck full of tools that he stored in the smokehouse.

Uncle Paul sent for his son, who lived with his divorced mother out West in California. Then we had two more people living at the Cross Ell, and it was fun to have a cousin to talk to. He was smart and knew movie stars and swam in the Pacific Ocean.

Uncle Paul took a corner lot in Four Sand where he could start a new business. He loaded the wagon at the Cameron Lumber Yard with bright new boards cut from sweet-smelling East Texas pine trees. Our mules, Babe and Pete, pulled the wagon out to Four Sand, and Uncle Paul and his son, Bruce Merril, unloaded it and built a brand new grocery store, the first one in the new town.

The storefront went up high and square. There were two rooms inside. The front part was filled with shelves for groceries and a counter to collect the money, and the back room was storage and space for two cots and a table where Uncle Paul and Bruce Merril lived. Out back they built a brand new "privy." There were three iron barrels, two for water and one for coal oil to use in lamps and cook stoves. They had everything they needed for a complete house and grocery store.

They painted a sign on the front that said "THE RISING SON GROCERY." Uncle Paul was proud of Bruce Merril, who did most of the work, building, cooking, cleaning, and selling groceries.

One day Bruce got tired of doing most of the work, so while his papa was off somewhere he got some white paint and painted over the name and made a new sign that said "SITTING BULL GROCERY."

When Uncle Paul came back he painted the whole front white and put the sign back to read "RISING SON GROCERY." The store looked even better with white paint behind the black letters.

The Rising Son Grocery was a keen place to visit while I was growing up. They had little wax bottles filled with colored syrup that sold for a penny. I could bite the top off the little bottle and suck out the sweet syrup, then chew the wax for hours afterward. There were punchboards with prizes to win and chewy chocolate soldiers wrapped in paper.

If you had a nickel, they sold Dr. Pepper soda pop — "Good at ten, two, and four o'clock." If there was ice in the cooler the drinks were cold, but if they were waiting for the ice man to come from Southern Ice Company twenty-five miles away, they were just wet on the outside.

Baby Sister loved the reddish-brown peanut patties washed down with an R.C. Cola. Uncle Paul would hold out a nickel in one hand and a dime in the other and tell us to pick the one we wanted and he would give it to us. She always picked the nickel. He laughed and told people in the store, "She picked the nickel because it is bigger than the dime."

Out back of the store I coached Baby Sister, "The dime was worth two nickels, and you should have chosen the dime! Don't be such a dummy!"

Baby Sister said, "No, if I choose the nickel he will do it again every time someone comes in the store."

That night Baby Sister had five nickels and I had my only dime!

Bruce Merril let me candle eggs. That is where you go in the back room where it is dark and hold the eggs one at the time over a hole in a cardboard box with a light in it. You can look through the shell to see if there are any baby chicks inside or cracks or blood spots. We returned any bad eggs to the ladies who brought them in and paid for the good ones at the rate of twelve cents a dozen in cash money or thirteen cents a dozen in trade.

If the ladies left the bad eggs, Bruce Merril and I fed them to cats that lived under the floor.

One day a man came in and said he wanted to buy the whole place, groceries and all. He gave Uncle Paul some money, and we went away and left it with him. He made a good deal because he got thirty-two cats he didn't even know he owned.

I was sad to see Uncle Paul and Bruce leave because I liked knowing a rich grocery store owner. I wished my Daddy would let me help him build a grocery store and maybe I could be the rising son. I don't know of any other kids who had a grocery store named after them just because they did nice things like building a house and store all together. There aren't many stores like the Rising Son Grocery these days.

RIDE NAKED IN THE MOONLIGHT

Growing up on the ranch taught lessons not found in school, like the one I learned riding naked in the moonlight. A school friend came on his sorrel horse to go camping with me. The Indian Summer weather was perfect, before the first frost. There was a full harvest moon, and our spirits were high.

We hurried through my evening chores, our thoughts turned to the "olden days" when Indians lived here and kids grew up free, without school or chores, riding, hunting, and following every whim and fancy.

Our camp site was on a mesa called South Mountain, some six miles away and one of the highest points in the county. It was covered with juniper, cactus, and mesquite, tilted upward to the limestone edge of the mesa ending in cliffs and a talus running east for several miles. Below the talus, canyons ran down to Sulfur Draw, and beyond it the high plains reached to the skyline.

We packed a canteen of water, apples, biscuits, and jerky, and as good Indians we left modern inventions, matches, and rifles at home. We talked so much about the "olden times" that the reality of distant train whistles in the freight yards and faraway twinkling lights of the town were erased from our minds, giving way to make-believe that keeps young minds busy.

A huge yellow harvest moon was rising beyond Signal Peak, east of South Mountain. Mourning doves called to newly arriving stars in a cloudless Indian Summer sky. We hobbled the horses, made our beds with saddles for pillows and blankets spread over buffalo grass. Being close to nature's wonders, we became two Indian boys a hundred years ago.

My friend commented, "Wouldn't it be great to live free like this all the time? We could ride our ponies without saddles or bridles, even ride naked in the moonlight along these cliffs."

The idea was daring, and since the horses were neither saddled nor bridled and we were nearly naked on our bedrolls, it took no effort to unhobble our mounts and swing up on their backs and shed our remaining clothes. We held on to the horses' flowing manes, and with their tails streaming out behind them, their steel shoes striking sparks on the rocks, we were actually riding naked in the moonlight.

The freedom of that moment lives on in the soul. Such things reach deep but don't last long. Horses tire and boys' attention is easily distracted. There was this little road, scarcely more than a track. On that road was a parked car, with a couple also enjoying the moonlight. They came to the mesa with their own thoughts of taking advantage of the moment and season.

If there is anything more exciting to young boys than an adventure, it's another adventure! We ate our apples down to the core, galloping along. In a moment of inspiration we thought how much fun it would be to toss our apple cores through the open window of that Ford coupe.

Silently we slipped from the ponies, allowing them to graze peacefully a little distance from the parked car. Like Indians, we moved through the moonlight close to the open window. One core went inside, the other splattered on the windshield.

We were shocked when the headlights came on and the motor started. Here were not two Indian braves, but two buck naked kids standing in the headlights of a moving car in the middle of a prairie full of sharp rocks, mesquite, juniper, and prickly pear cactus. My friend caught his pony's mane, swung his back, and was away like the wind, leaning on the neck to present a low profile. My own pony was right beside him, also going like the wind, and without me!

It was then that I learned another important lifetime lesson: Indians may have ridden their ponies naked in the moonlight, but naked or not they never took off their moccasins!

Bare feet, sharp rocks, cactus, and naked bodies can leave some nasty scars when they come together in a moonlight race.

The chase was short. By running between large boulders I could go where the car would not follow. The Ford turned around and disappeared into the night — and one make-believe Indian was ready to return to civilization with leather boots, saddles, clothes, and modern day inventions.

Riding naked in the moonlight was an adventure, but the reason we have modern things is because they are better. Reliving the "olden days" lets us appreciate what we now have. Once having ridden naked in the moonlight, one never forgets and there is no need to try it again.

WHAT I LEARNED ON THE RANCH

We learned all those things on the ranch, before we ever moved to town.

Close gates behind you if they were closed when you came to them, and leave them open if you found them that way. Watch out for wasp nests, snakes, and spiders. Respect your elders. Save your money, and pay back what you borrow.

Take a good look at things every day. Watch a spider make a web, an ant digging a hole, or a sky filled with stars. Watch a calf get its dinner, or pigs lolling in the mud. Notice how horses sweat around the collar when they work, let them rest before you work them some more, and see them roll in the dust when you take their harness off.

Swing in an old automobile tire hanging from a mesquite tree limb. Listen to the wind as it turns the tin windmill and hear how it pings, then listen to the same wind turning the wooden windmill and hear it make another sound from the same wind. Watch the mockingbird proclaim his territory from the tip of the lightning rod on the smoke house.

Take two biscuits, poke your finger in, and fill the holes with syrup. Eat one with milk and stuff the other in your

pocket for later. Don't sit on it. Never gather eggs in your pocket and crawl through a corral fence.

Never shoot anything you don't intend to cook and eat, unless it's trying to eat your plants or animals. All guns should be treated as loaded and dangerous, and never as toys. Don't point at things you don't intend to shoot and kill. Learn to shoot straight and clean, never cripple.

Learn something new every day. Think. Talk to people and hear what they think. Ask questions and listen, really listen, without saying a word yourself. Read and take care of books.

Every day work a little — chop weeds, plant seeds, feed the chickens, water the flowers in pots, carry the milk buckets to the corrals, toss bundles of red-top cane from the barn loft down to the mules. Give your horse some maize heads to eat from your hand. Squirt cows' milk on the faces of the cats that follow you to the milk pens and see them lick it off nice and clean.

Hang up your clothes, scrape the mud off your boots before you go to bed, and say your prayers before you go to sleep, before you eat, and sometimes in between.

Before you drift off to sleep, take time to wonder: How did God make every blade of grass that ripples like water in a pond when the wind blows? Every tiny mesquite leaf and bean? How did he teach the birds to build nests, warm the eggs until they hatch, trust the air enough to launch themselves from their lofty homes and fly away? How do the long-legged sand hill cranes know the way to Canada and back to the Cross Ell Ranch again? How did he make all those pretty stars?

It's not for me to know how, just to know that He did it all, and He looks over me as I sleep, and He takes care of me all my life and even when I die. It's nice to have a friend like Him who cares about people, because mostly people don't care enough about each other.

We planted a sweet potato in a jar of water, and it grew vines on the windowsill. We caught baby rabbits, making snug homes for them of sand and grass and a lid of water. We caught doodle bugs and put them in jars and watched them make their cone-shaped ant traps. The baby rabbits died, and the doodle bugs, and the potato vine. They all die, and we do, too. But that's not the end. Each year in springtime, the new life comes back again.

How nice it would be if everyone in the world would follow some simple basic rules. Instead, folks make things hard when it's not really for us to figure out for ourselves. We need to know that all is well. Have faith in His word, and enjoy what there is to enjoy. Sing a little, dance some, play, work, sleep. Learn to say "I love you" to those we love, and never stop saying it. It won't wear out.

I Give You a Star

My dad originally presented this story to the family at Christmas. Since his passing, there has been a tradition of giving each other stars, in some token or another, at Christmas. Of all his stories, this certainly ranks as our favorite. –Don Frazier

—

There was so much land, so much sky, and few people to talk to. At night when it was dark, the sky spread all the way over us, beyond the Cross Ell Ranch, clear to where it touches the ground in every direction.

In school we read about interesting things, and when I came home there was no one to share them with, so I thought and thought about what I had learned. Some day I might get to tell people about it. I thought about some things they didn't teach me, but by putting them together I got new ideas.

In October we studied about Christopher Columbus, who discovered the New World – America. It was an exciting lesson, but it was not exactly a new discovery because there were people here before Columbus found it. He thought he was in India, so he called those people Indians.

Maybe they thought they discovered Columbus, because neither of them knew about the other before October twelve in fourteen hundred and ninety two when they discovered each other.

My teacher said Columbus sighted land and left his ship to come to the shore. When he got to the beach he spread his arms out wide and said in a loud voice, "I claim these lands for the queen!"

He set the flag and a Christian cross in the sand, and after that all the land was supposed to belong to Isabella of Spain, who probably never set foot on the lands he had given her in that little speech. Still, Spain owned a lot of new territory because of what Columbus said and did.

Well, I had a lot of time to think about that in the night time as I looked up into the Milky Way. That's the big strip of stars that reaches clear across the sky, and there are so many of them that I'll bet you never could count them all.

Looking up night after night, the thought came to me that nobody has ever claimed all those beautiful stars. I reasoned, "All the stars up there are free for the taking."

The more I thought about it the more I liked the idea of claiming them, all of them, hundreds and millions of them. They would all be mine, and I could do whatever I wanted with them because I'd be owner of the stars.

Columbus planted a flag when he claimed America, and I didn't know how to get a flag up there even if I had a flag. Then as I thought about it, it was almost like Sam, my on-duty guardian angel, whispered in my ear, "Son, you've got a flag. It's right up there in the sky just waiting for you to do something about it. See, it's the Cross Ell!"

Sure enough, I could see a cross with a star off beside it in the shape of the Cross Ell cattle brand. I was so excited that I ran a little way out from the house where I could see all the sky everywhere. It made little shivers go down my back looking at it and thinking about what I was about to do.

I spread my arms and said in the biggest little-boy voice I could manage, "I claim all the stars in the sky as mine, mine, mine, by my right to unclaimed lands, and I take possession of it for God, my king. I own it, and there to prove it is our cattle brand, the Cross Ell, made out of stars for the world to see."

No one was listening unless it was Sam, and he didn't talk and no one ever saw him, so it was just like a secret. It was a secret I never forgot, and I'm telling it to you right now. I own all the stars in the sky, and I have for all the time since that wonderful night when I laid claim to them all.

I didn't claim the moon because that was too big and close, and I thought someone just might have claimed it before me, and I didn't want any arguments over ownership. I didn't claim the sun either, because to tell the truth I was so excited about owning all the stars I didn't even think about it in the dark. The sun was out of sight and out of mind when this great event took place.

Years have passed since I made my claim and to this day no one has disputed it, so I think maybe I really do own all the stars.

They fascinated me, and since I owned them, I figured I had better get to know them better, like riding over a new range to see what grew there. I found out that twinkling stars were really suns that may have planets circling them as our sun does. Then the planets probably have moons circling them, too.

Planets don't generate light but only reflect it, so you can't really see them from so far away, but Albert and Sam agree that they are really truly out there. Roscoe would say the same thing, only he was off duty about then.

I finally realized that no one really knows what all is included in my universe of stars, no more than Columbus and his queen knew what all was in the lands he claimed for Spain. He didn't know about the Mississippi River, the Grand Canyon, or even Texas. It was all there when he claimed it, and he didn't even know.

It was grand to be the owner of so vast a property. Then it was sad, because no one knew my secret. Such a wonderful thing has to be shared with others to bring full joy to the owner. I think that's the very reason God made mankind — to share the earth he had created, to bring full joy to God.

I know He owns the stars, I just laid claim to them as his servant, like Columbus claimed the New World for Queen Isabella.

Years passed and I have found owning all the stars is a lot more than one person can enjoy, so I thought about sharing them with others. I picked out one star in particular, where the Bar crosses the Ell in the cattle brand. That is my special star, and I shall keep it forever, even when I have passed on to where the buffalo and wooly mammoths have gone. That special star will still be mine.

Now that I have chosen my own star, I'm setting about giving the rest of them away. I have so many I can give them to all nice people I meet and still have lots and lots of them left over. So I invite you to choose a star for yourself.

Now, when you pick one out, tell me where it is as I have told you how to locate mine. This way I shall always be able to look at your star and remember you, and you may do the same with mine. Our friendship will endure so long as those two stars shine in the midnight sky.

They will twinkle up there together when you and I are both gone from this earth. Folks who know this story will see our stars and remember we were everlasting friends.

This is the best use I can think of for the stars I have claimed. Remember it was a star that belonged to the Christ Child that brought kings and shepherds to the manger where he was born. Though I claimed the stars, I know they all belong to God, but for now I, like Columbus, have claimed them to put them to use in the cause of friendship.

You must go out into the star-filled night and choose your own. Take your time, mark it well, and tell me where it is, so you and I will always be together in the stars, no matter how far away we wander, one from the other. Take one of my stars as your special gift at Christmas, place its likeness on top of your Christmas tree, and remember the baby Jesus, then go outside in the night and look at our two stars, high in the sky.

That special star is yours forever. Help me give them all away to all your friends until every living person has his own friendship star, for as long as Christmas stars shall shine.

I'll do the same and think of you, while you think of me.